Activities for including chi

Cognitive
and learning
difficulties

IDENTIFYING NEEDS • INCLUSIVE ACTIVITY IDEAS • ASSESSMENT ADVICE • PLANNING INTERVENTIONS

SCHOLASTIC

DR HANNAH MORTIMER AND EILEEN JONES

Authors
Dr Hannah Mortimer
Eileen Jones

Editor
Victoria Lee

Assistant Editor
Catherine Gilhooly

Series Designers
Sarah Rock/Anna Oliwa

Designers
Melissa Leeke/Erik Ivens

Illustrations
Shelagh McNicholas

Cover artwork
Claire Henley

Acknowledgements
David Higham Associates for the use of an extract from
Lola Rose by Jacqueline Wilson © 2003, Jacqueline Wilson (2003, Doubleday).
Every effort has been made to trace copyright holders and the publishers apologise for any
inadvertent omissions.
Due to the nature of the web, the publisher cannot guarantee the content of the links of
any of the websites referred to. It is the responsibility of the reader to assess the suitability
of websites.

Text © 2006, Hannah Mortimer, Eileen Jones
© 2006, Scholastic Ltd

Published by Scholastic Ltd, Villiers House,
Clarendon Avenue, Leamington Spa, Warwickshire CV32 5PR

Visit our website at www.scholastic.co.uk

Printed by Bell & Bain Ltd, Glasgow

1 2 3 4 5 6 7 8 9 0   6 7 8 9 0 1 2 3 4 5

British Library Cataloguing-in-Publication Data A catalogue record for this book is
available from the British Library.

ISBN 0-439-96533-0   ISBN 978-0439-96533-0

Activities for including children with cognitive and learning difficulties

INTRODUCTION

Including children who have cognition and learning needs can be both challenging and rewarding. This book helps you put inclusion into practice so that all the children benefit.

Aims of the series

The Code of Practice for the identification and assessment of special educational needs (DfES) gives guidance on including children who have disabilities and other special educational needs (SEN) in England. In addition, the National Numeracy and National Literacy Strategies emphasise the key role that teachers play in making sure that the curriculum is accessible to all pupils. The Government's strategy for SEN includes a whole framework of initiatives to remove barriers to pupils' achievement and we are now beginning to see joined up policies that can make real differences to children. This series aims to provide suggestions to class teachers and others working in schools on how to meet and monitor SEN under the new guidelines. It provides accessible information and advice for class teachers and subject teachers at Key Stage 1 and Key Stage 2. It also provides practical examples of how teachers can use this information to plan inclusive teaching across the strands of the National Curriculum.

There is related legislation and guidance in Wales, Scotland and Northern Ireland though the detail and terminology is rather different. For example, the Statement of SEN in England and Wales is called a Record in Scotland. Nevertheless, the general approaches and information covered in this book will be relevant throughout the UK. Within this *Special Needs in the Primary Years* series, there are books on helping children with most kinds of special educational need:

● *Special Needs Handbook*, which supplies general information for special educational needs coordinators (SENCOs) or class teachers to help meet all the SEN in the school or class
● *The Essential A–Z Guide to Special Needs*, which provides basic information for class teachers and support assistants
● *Activities for Including Children with Behavioural Difficulties*
● *Activities for Including Children with Autistic Spectrum Difficulties*
● *Activities for Including Children with Dyslexia and Language Difficulties*
● *Activities for Including Children with Cognitive and Learning Difficulties*.
The last four titles contain practical activities for including children with these kinds of SEN in the primary curriculum.

The children concerned

This book aims to provide a broad understanding of what it means to have cognition and learning needs and to show how primary teachers can plan individual approaches for these children. Sometimes, you know of a medical cause why a child might have cognition or learning needs and you will meet some of these conditions in Chapter 1. However, for most children identified as having general learning needs,

there will be no known cause. Perhaps they have not yet had all the opportunities that they need in order to learn. Others may lack the confidence to learn or have not yet been presented with a curriculum that suits their learning style or strengths. It does not matter what might have caused the difficulty in the past. Your task as a teacher is to identify the fact that a child might be learning differently to others and to provide all the right opportunities and support for that child. This is an exciting challenge and, with careful planning, you should all be able to celebrate success at each individual child's level, step by small step.

Who this book is for
First and foremost, this book is for SENCOs, class teachers and support assistants who work on a daily basis with the children. The book will also be helpful for support professionals, headteachers and governors to use with the staff they work with. The SENCO's role is to support their colleagues in meeting SEN in their schools, though it is the responsibility of each staff member to support children who have SEN within their classes. This book will help SENCOs provide colleagues with general information about identifying, assessing, planning for and including children in their classes who have cognition and learning needs. Finally, the book will also be a useful reference for parents, carers and trainees.

Looking for inclusive opportunities
There seem to be certain common features that promote inclusion.
● There is usually careful joint planning. For example, if there is special support for a child, how will it be used? Will the child still have access to the same range of adults, children and activities as any other child in the group would?
● Staff use educational labels rather than categories or medical labels (such as 'learning difficulty' rather than 'educationally subnormal' or 'mentally handicapped', or even 'a child who has SEN' rather than 'a SEN child').
● Teachers and adults provide good role models for the children because of their positive expectations and the way they respect and value the children.
● Special attention is given to improving children's language and communication skills.
● Teaching strategies are developed which enable *all* children to participate and to learn.
● Individual approaches are planned which draw on pupils' earlier experiences, set high expectations and encourage mutual peer support.
● There is a flexible use of support aimed at promoting joining in and inclusion rather than creating barriers and exclusion.

How to use this book
In Chapter 1 you will be introduced to the concept of 'inclusion' as it relates to children with cognition and learning needs. In particular, you will see what the implications of these difficulties are for the child and for the teacher at different ages and stages. You will also think about

some of the issues and challenges that you face when working with these children. There are suggestions for assessing children with different kinds of learning difficulties in Chapter 2. Sometimes different types of difficulty might call for different types of assessment and you will be helped to select the most appropriate method for your situation. You will also find a description of the legal requirements you have to identify and support children who have SEN on account of their cognition and learning needs. Chapter 3 helps you to plan interventions for these children, working with their strengths and weaknesses. You will meet a wide range of approaches that colleagues in other schools have found helpful and you will later be helped to match these approaches effectively to your teaching activities.

Six activity chapters follow and these cover the six strands of the National Curriculum which are perhaps affected most by this area of need. If a child has a significant difficulty in cognition and learning, then most will have experienced difficulties in acquiring basic literacy skills. They are therefore likely to experience difficulties in the areas of English 1: Speaking and listening, English 2: Reading and English 3: Writing. Children with cognitive difficulties might also find Mathematics 1: Using and applying mathematics and Science 1: Scientific enquiry challenging, especially as topics become more complex and abstract. They might also have difficulties with the understanding and the recording side of humanities and the strand of History has been chosen to serve as an example.

Though there may well be learning difficulties across each strand, it is hoped that examples in these six areas of the curriculum will provide you with the starting points and ideas necessary for helping you deliver the entire curriculum in a supportive and inclusive way. There are two teaching activities for each age range of five to seven years, seven to nine years and nine to eleven years, each on a separate page. You will also find an introduction to each strand, covering how children with cognition and learning needs are likely to be affected in that particular strand of the curriculum. This links back to Chapter 2 and allows you to select the most appropriate methods of assessment and observation.

For each teaching activity, you will find a 'Learning objective for all the children' and also an 'Individual learning target' for children with cognition and learning needs. There are also suggestions for 'Extension' (what to try if the targets were met) and for providing 'Special support' for the child with SEN. The support suggestions link back to Chapter 3 where each approach is described to you in more detail. The activities have been selected to make a particular point for teaching children with cognition and learning needs, reflecting the strengths, weaknesses, opportunities and challenges of those pupils. The activities should be adapted to suit the situation of each teacher and class, and should act as a stimulus to trigger ideas.

Throughout the book there are photocopiable pages linked to assessment, monitoring and planning the activities and, at the end of the book, there is a list of helpful resources. You will find more detail about meeting SEN in the book *Special Needs Handbook* by Hannah Mortimer (Scholastic), also from this series.

Setting the scene

The activities described in this book encourage you to make use of a wide range of resources, materials and learning environments available in your school. Special use is made of differentiated approaches since these have been shown to be effective in including children with cognition and learning needs. There are also activities that help children 'learn how to learn'. The approaches have all been selected to make the child feel positive about their learning experiences and therefore grow in confidence.

In just the same way, as staff members, you need to be confident if you are to cope with the very individual approach that children with significant learning difficulties sometimes need. The learning activities you plan should involve strategies for supporting these children that are workable and effective and should leave staff and children alike feeling positive.

If you skim through the entire book first, focusing especially on the curriculum introductions and on the ideas for support, you will pick up ideas which you can transfer to different situations and different curriculum strands. After that, you may find it best to dip into the book as necessary, using it as flexibly as you need to.

Links with home

The SEN *Code of Practice* has strengthened the importance of 'parent partnership' and of good communication and joint planning between school and home. Where a child's cognition and learning needs are such that you need approaches that are *additional to* or *different from* usual, then you need to place their names on the school's SEN approaches and take School Action. This means that you will need to set and review a regular individual education plan. In this case, you are obliged to involve parents and carers fully in the process. It is not always easy talking to parents and carers about their child's difficulties. You may find this easier if you can discuss some of the activities and approaches you are doing in class and share the ideas for target setting, support and extension which are exemplified in this book.

OVERVIEW GRID FOR AGES 5–7

ACTIVITY TITLE	SUBJECT	INDIVIDUAL TARGET	LEARNING OBJECTIVE	OUTCOME
Story time	Speaking and listening	To look at the teacher, listen and respond to group instructions.	To listen and follow instructions accurately.	The children take parts in a retelling of a story.
What a performance!	Speaking and listening	To speak or communicate in a simple role play.	To adopt appropriate roles in small groups.	Familiar stories are a starting point for improvised dialogue and role play.
Pond fishing	Reading	To identify key words from a reader.	To read on sight high frequency words specific to graded books matched to the abilities of reading groups.	Words written on paper fish are 'caught' and then read by the children in order to win the game.
Sound searchers	Reading	To hear the initial letter sound within a word.	To secure identification, spelling and reading of initial sounds in simple words.	Initial letter sounds are learned in a variety of games.
Which way?	Writing	To trace an anticlockwise circle in the sand.	To form lower-case letters correctly in a script.	The children learn how letters are formed through fun activities.
Words in print	Writing	To print their name in different fonts or colours on the computer.	To use simple poetry structures and to substitute own ideas and write new lines.	Computers are used to enable the children to present their own poetry.
Mighty more and little less	Using and applying mathematics	To understand what is meant by more than and less than.	To understand and use the vocabulary of comparing and ordering numbers.	Concrete and fun activities teach the children more than and less than.
Count the problems!	Using and applying mathematics	To use counting to solve practical problems.	To use mental addition and subtraction, simple multiplication and division to solve simple word problems involving numbers in 'real life'.	The children solve practical mathematical problems which are based on their school day.
Get moving!	Scientific enquiry	To copy simple movements and use action words to describe them.	To observe and describe different ways of moving.	Movements are practised and described in a PE session.
Spot the difference	Scientific enquiry	To cooperate within a small team in presenting simple evidence to others.	To learn that some differences between ourselves and other children can be measured.	Graphs are created to show comparisons between the children.
A lady with a lamp	History	To take part in a themed activity linked to Florence Nightingale.	To learn about some of the improvements made by Florence Nightingale, and to identify some reasons for her actions.	The children role play different aspects of Florence Nightingale's life.
Seaside memories	History	To use or respond to language in the past tense.	To find out about seaside holidays in the past by asking questions of an adult visitor.	A pretend visitor allows the children to consider seaside holidays of the past.

OVERVIEW GRID FOR AGES 7–9

ACTIVITY TITLE	SUBJECT	INDIVIDUAL TARGET	LEARNING OBJECTIVE	OUTCOME
A magic wand	Speaking and listening	To take a turn in a speaking and listening activity during circle time.	To make contributions, speaking audibly and listening actively.	Everyone is involved in a discussion about a fund-raising event.
Elephants always remember	Speaking and listening	To use a simple mnemonic to remember the order of information.	To use language to structure information.	The children make up their own mnemonics.
Scrambled sentences	Reading	To assemble individual word cards in order to build up a sentence.	To write in complete sentences.	Complete sentences are created from assembling individual words.
Remind me again	Reading	To refer to a written list in order to get organised for the school day.	To write instructions.	The children write their own aides-mémoires.
What happens to your Cinderella?	Writing	To write a simple sentence independently.	To write alternative sequels to traditional stories.	A traditional story is rewritten by the children.
Fantasyland	Writing	To plan a short independent piece or writing using a mind map.	To understand how writers create imaginary worlds.	Mind maps are used to help in the creation of a piece of writing.
That's a mistake!	Using and applying mathematics	To 'mark' and correct a simple piece of written mathematics.	To check subtraction with addition.	The children learn how addition can be used to check subtraction sums.
Eat your money's worth	Using and applying mathematics	To respond to a simple problem-solving task using multiple choice.	To use all four operations to solve word problems in 'real life'.	The children work out how best to spend £5 from a café menu.
Pet questions	Scientific enquiry	To ask a simple question and find out an answer.	To raise key questions about the diet of different pets.	Small groups work together to research and present information about pets.
Testing temperatures	Scientific enquiry	To read a thermometer.	To make careful measurements of temperature at regular time intervals.	An experiment on how to keep a drink warm teaches children about temperature and insulation.
Time lines	History	To use a simple time line to sequence events.	To learn how many times Henry VIII married.	The children create a time line for Henry VIII and his wives.
The Vikings are here!	History	To work with a partner in collecting data via a website.	To conduct a Viking case study.	Websites are used to help research a project about the Vikings.

OVERVIEW GRID FOR AGES 9–11

ACTIVITY TITLE	SUBJECT	INDIVIDUAL TARGET	LEARNING OBJECTIVE	OUTCOME
Words can count	Speaking and listening	To read from a prepared report.	To use a range of oral techniques to present a persuasive argument.	The children propose a change to the school in a speech.
Any questions... any answers?	Speaking and listening	To use descriptive language with a partner.	To use and explore different question types. To practise and extend vocabulary.	A game where the children guess hidden objects through the use of description.
Rave reviews	Reading	To select and read a book, reporting back on why it was enjoyable.	To evaluate a book by referring to details and examples in the text. To analyse the features of a good opening.	The children review stories or the opening chapters of novels.
Cartoon stories	Reading	To draw a simple cartoon to represent the main sequence of a written story.	To write summaries of books or parts of books, deciding on priorities relevant to purpose.	The children create their own cartoon from a book extract.
Model manuscripts	Writing	To make careful pen movements in a simple illumination.	To use the structures of poems read to write extensions based on these.	Careful presentation of written work is encouraged in the children's poems.
Buried treasure	Writing	To write a simple sequence of instructions with support.	To revise the language conventions and grammatical features of instructional texts.	The children give each other instructions to find 'buried treasure'.
Channel choice chance	Using and applying mathematics	To work as part of a team, gathering data.	To discuss the chance or likelihood of certain events.	The children pick coloured coins at random to disprove a given hypothesis.
Shopping spree	Using and applying mathematics	To contribute to complex problem-solving, step by small step.	To identify and use appropriate operations to solve word problems involving numbers and quantities.	Receipts from a shopping trip lead the children to solve different mathematical problems.
Finger on the pulse	Scientific enquiry	To work with a partner to log simple data using ICT.	To learn how to measure their pulse rate and relate it to heartbeat.	The children create graphs of their pulse rates.
What can you see?	Scientific enquiry	To observe and talk about a simple effect.	To make and record comparisons of how different surfaces reflect light and to draw conclusions from their comparisons.	Shiny and dull surfaces are explored in a practical experiment to show reflection.
Memory mind maps	History	To work with an adult to produce a mind map about the Victorians.	To find out about important figures in Victorian times and to present their findings in different ways.	The children make mind maps of the life of Queen Victoria.
Time travellers	History	To collect information about an event that happened in the past.	To learn in what ways the modern Olympic games are like the ancient ones.	Group research enables the children to ask and answer questions on the Olympic games.

INCLUDING CHILDREN WITH COGNITIVE AND LEARNING DIFFICULTIES

In this chapter we explore what is meant by 'cognitive and learning difficulties'. There are practical suggestions for making the primary curriculum more accessible for these children.

About cognitive and learning difficulties

The activities in this book are targeted mainly at children who have a general delay in their development and learning. Sometimes, you may hear these difficulties described as 'cognitive difficulties' or '*general* learning difficulties'. It makes sense to consider a child's learning in the context of a wide continuum covering how *all* children learn and develop. Some children achieve their developmental milestones ahead of most other children their age. Some children achieve their milestones later than others. Somewhere along this continuum, we might decide that a child is learning and progressing out of line with their peers and that we should adopt additional and different approaches to encourage their progress. These are the children who have SEN on account of their cognition and learning needs.

Causes and effects

There are a few children where it is obvious that there are *risks* of general learning difficulties from birth. For example, children with Down's syndrome usually have a greater difficulty learning than the majority of children their age. The word 'syndrome' means a collection of signs and characteristics. All people with Down's syndrome have certain facial and other physical characteristics, which make them appear similar. However, it is important to realise that there are far more differences between people with Down's syndrome than similarities. Each child is an individual in their own right and we need to recognise this.

One baby in about 1000 is born with Down's syndrome. It is caused by an additional chromosome in each body cell. People with Down's syndrome have 47 chromosomes instead of the usual 46. This results in the development of the growing baby in the womb becoming disrupted and altered. The chances of a baby being born with Down's syndrome increases with the mother's age, particularly over the age of 35. This is one of the reasons why older mothers are screened during pregnancy. Many children with Down's syndrome are healthy, but 40 per cent have heart problems at birth and some might need surgery. There is also a much higher risk of hearing difficulties, vision needs careful monitoring and there is a tendency towards more frequent infections and 'chestiness' too.

For other children with general learning difficulties, there might have been a medical cause very early in pregnancy or after birth. Perhaps there was some damage to the developing brain, or perhaps the conditions in the womb were not ideal because of other factors.

Sometimes children affected in this way can have profound and multiple learning difficulties in which all their senses and abilities remain at an early stage of development. There are also a few medical conditions to do with the body chemistry that can contribute to learning difficulties. Some early childhood illnesses, if serious enough, can also leave a child with developmental delay.

But for most children identified as having general learning difficulties, there will be no known cause. Perhaps they have not yet had all the opportunities that they need to be taught and to learn. Perhaps their self-esteem is very low and they lack confidence. Perhaps, on the continuum of how all children develop, they seem to need longer time than other children their age to acquire new learning. It does not matter what caused the difficulty in the past. Your task in your class is to identify the fact that a child might be learning differently to others and to provide all the right opportunities and support to bring that child on. This is an exciting challenge and, with careful planning, you should all be delighted to celebrate success, step by small step.

This step-by-step approach is central to helping children who have learning needs. Your task is not to 'fix' a learning difficulty as if it were a medical condition. Your task is to identify it and to plan the appropriate support to remove any barriers to learning, either yourself or with the help of outside agencies. If you start to think in terms of planning and celebrating progress rather than 'fixing', then you, the child and the parents will all come to feel much more positive about how your teaching is progressing.

Sometimes you will find that the very fact that you have identified a gap in a child's knowledge and understanding, and have planned an approach to help, will mean that the gap no longer exists. Suddenly, the child will be doing all the same learning activities that most other children their age are doing. That child no longer has a learning difficulty. Other times you will find that a child will always have a need for specially planned and supported activities, and you will continue to differentiate the curriculum you are offering.

Do not hold back from thinking in terms of special needs, if your extra input is going to make a real difference. The fact that you are putting into place special approaches does not label the child and create the problem; it could actually prevent the problem from being there. It is for this reason that we are asked to see the SEN *Code of Practice* very flexibly, adopting it from time to time with children who might have a real need at any one stage for that little bit extra in terms of our careful planning and input. If we provide a differentiated and flexible curriculum, then we can truly hope to include all children's needs within our schools. You will find many ideas for differentiating the curriculum in Chapter 3.

Developmental delay

All children vary widely in the age at which they reach various developmental stages, such as lacing their shoes, knowing their letters and numbers, or balancing on one leg. It is quite normal to have a wide variation in your class. However, some children fail to

achieve their developmental milestones within the usual time range and are sometimes described as being 'delayed' in their development. Sometimes you may be working with children who are *globally* delayed in their development – in their language and communication, their motor skills, their self-help skills, their ability to socialise and their cognitive skills. You will need extremely flexible approaches to ensure that these pupils are included in each strand of the curriculum and you will certainly need to make reference to the QCA P scales when setting targets for these pupils (see page 25). In older children, developmental delay manifests itself in the child attaining National Curriculum levels normally but at a slower pace than most of the other children in the class. Some children will catch up eventually; others may continue to have learning difficulties. The help that you should provide is the same.

What you can do

● Use a phased intervention following the guidance of the SEN *Code of Practice* (Chapter 2). The level of support does not depend on the label (for example, whether the child has Down's syndrome) but on how the child progresses and the additional or different approaches that you need to put into place to help them learn.

● Children with global developmental delay need individually planned programmes of work aimed at developing their motor skills, their language and communication and their ability to help themselves, as well as in whichever strand of the National Curriculum you are working.

● Make sure that you moderate your expectations so that the child has the chance of learning through success, whatever the developmental level.

● Plan any additional support carefully so that the child is not socially isolated – socialising might be their strongest area of ability and this strength can be built on.

● Always be aware of the child's developmental level in each area – if a child is using language appropriate to a five-year-old then this is where your intervention must start, even if that child has motor or social skills at a much higher level.

● Children with global developmental delay need plenty of repetition in order to learn new skills, but they will quickly become bored if you offer the same activity over and over. Look for new ways of teaching the same skills, for example, tracing over letter shapes, hand-painting letter shapes, handling solid letter shapes, playing with magnetic letters.

● From time to time, you may suspect that progress has come to a halt. Children do 'plateau' from time to time and this is not unusual. You might also see some regression if there has been a hospital stay, an illness or if the child has suffered a severe epileptic episode. Expect to revisit and review earlier teaching targets if this happens, even if you felt you had successfully completed them earlier.

● Children with global delay often need time to respond. Get to know the child well so that you can reduce distraction and adapt to their pace.

- Always make sure that you know how the child communicates their feelings, moods and needs. Even if the child cannot use words, you can interpret behaviour and expression and help others to do so too, perhaps making use of an illustrated communication book (for example, 'This is how Liam looks when he is ready to move on to a new activity').
- Keep story times and discussion times simple by using concrete props for the child to look at and handle.
- Emphasise key words and keep your language simple and clear.
- Establish eye contact before speaking in order to engage the child's attention fully.
- Encourage the development of all three learning styles (visual, auditory and kinaesthetic) by using multi-sensory approaches (approaches which involve seeing, listening and doing).
- Keep activities short and end on a successful note.
- Use your praise and encouragement to make the child feel successful when learning.
- Look for opportunities in which the child *needs* to communicate, by offering choices and encouraging initiative. In other words, try to avoid the *learned helplessness* that can develop when everything is provided 'on a plate'.
- Use a structured step-by-step approach for teaching new developmental skills, such as putting on a coat, telling the time or developing independent writing. Step in and help only at those moments when the child cannot manage. Encourage the child to be as independent as possible and proud of it too.
- Use small groups and circles to encourage language and listening.
- Provide materials that make it possible for that child to participate fully (for example, triangular pen holds for immature writing, squeezy scissors, concrete counting aids and number lines to assist basic mathematics, easier tasks and activities).

Independence training

Children with cognition and learning needs often need extra encouragement and support to develop initiative, independence and persistence in their learning. They may have more difficulties than others in acquiring independence skills, perhaps because their hands are still clumsy, they have short attention spans, or they cannot plan ahead so well. Children with cognition and learning needs may require your help, patience and encouragement to develop age-appropriate self-help skills. Though it is tempting to feel that these skills should have been taught early on, sometimes children are not developmentally ready to learn them until they are older.

What you can do

- You may notice that some of your older children are still very reliant on a parent or carer to organise them and, as a result, lack initiative and the ability to organise themselves. Encourage all the adults involved to 'step back a little' and encourage rather than take over. This will help to prevent 'learned helplessness'.
- When you are planning for SEN, have a mind to the children's

futures as well as the National Curriculum. In other words, plan for their independence, personal, social and emotional skills as well as the standard curriculum areas.

● Learn to provide just the right amount of help, and no more, to the child for whom you are teaching independence skills.

● Allow plenty of time for a child with disabilities to dress or undress independently and stay close to encourage and celebrate success.

● Think ahead about the independence skills necessary for Key Stage 3 (such as personal organisation, time management and study skills) and break these down into manageable steps, which you can teach the child before transfer.

● Teach step by step and then chain the steps together so that the child is managing more complex tasks.

● Try to give the children choices wherever possible, and set up situations so that they can exercise their ability to be as independent as possible at school.

● Encourage children to help each other.

● Use Key Stages 1 and 2 to make sure that the children 'learn how to learn' as well as what to learn (Chapter 2).

● Introduce multi-sensory study skills (such as mind mapping, mnemonics and thought storming) for all children, and especially those with learning difficulties.

● Think through the independence skills of all the children: toilets need to be accessible and welcoming, wash basins reachable, craft materials and technology equipment easy to reach, and choices given for activities wherever possible.

Concentration and attention

Children who have cognition and learning needs tend to have difficulties in paying attention and concentrating and may need particular support in developing these skills. Concentration and

attention in all children appear to develop over four areas. First, a child must learn to control attention, turning towards a familiar sound or looking towards a preferred friend or carer. Then children must learn to adapt their attention to a broad or narrow focus as needed, perhaps engaging in an activity but also being able to notice if it is playtime or if Mum has arrived. Later still, children must learn to plan their attention, deciding in advance what they are going to pay attention to and being able to cut out distractions that get in the way of the process. Finally they must learn to extend their attention and to concentrate for longer periods of time. Their preferred learning style will also play a part in their attention systems. If they learn primarily through *doing* rather than listening, you are bound to see them easily distracted by things to touch and fiddle with. It makes sense to build on this strength where appropriate (using multi-sensory teaching) or to remove distractions if you have to.

Exploration and learning

Children who have cognition and learning needs also need your support to develop initiative, exploration and problem-solving. Problem-solving occurs when children figure out how to use available materials or resources to achieve a goal. Both experience and developmental age contribute to this ability and you might find that a child with cognition and learning needs is slow to initiate and to make active choices in their learning and play. Children who have had past experience of playing with learning tools and resources (perhaps at nursery or pre-school) tend to solve learning problems more quickly than those who do not. Similarly, children who have cognition and learning needs will often benefit from the opportunity of sensory and exploratory play within their school day.

How does cooperative problem-solving typically develop? Direct observations of children in the early stages of cognition and development show that they engage mostly in solitary play, in which

they pay no attention to their peers, or in parallel play, in which they play next to each other but do not interact. As it develops, learning and play typically become more associative (in which children play together but not in a coordinated manner) or cooperative (in which children share a goal or mutual roles). Most children seek out and enjoy their peers. If they find themselves on their own, they will tend to join an ongoing group or activity. Over the primary school years, there are sharp increases in the strength of children's attachment to peers generally, and social relationships, particularly within gender, become closer, more frequent and sustained. Also, as development progresses, children become more willing to participate in joint efforts, coordinate their activities more effectively, and often collaborate successfully in solving problems.

Confidence and self-esteem

It is also true that children who have secure parental attachments have an advantage in the confidence this gives them to explore both their physical and their social worlds. One of the occasional repercussions of early medical problems leading to developmental difficulties can be that early attachments were interrupted by frequent hospitalisations. Children with learning difficulties inevitably suffer low self-esteem and poor confidence and sometimes take a lot of convincing and encouragement to see themselves as successful learners. Therefore you might need to focus on building children's confidences and attachments in class as well as meeting their cognitive and learning needs.

It is possible to observe the child whose self-esteem is low. Quite often you will notice certain characteristics and patterns of behaviour, though they are not a fixed rule. Of course, we all feel 'up' and 'down' on particular days, depending on recent events, our general sense of well-being, our health and our moods. Children, too, have their 'good days' and their 'bad days'.

Children who have low self-esteem often have a strong need for reassurance and often appear to feel insecure or 'prickly'. They have a low opinion of themselves, little faith in their own capabilities and easily become tearful when things go wrong. Sometimes they tend to over-react to failure and find it hard to accept correction. Sometimes they seem to feel safer if they 'take control' and you might find that they are frequently 'testing boundaries' or dominating other children's learning and play. They might tend to hurt or bully others.

What you can do

● Use a warm, positive approach with each child and invest individual time in your relationship. A key-worker system for vulnerable children in which one member of staff is responsible for befriending and supporting certain children can be helpful.
● Positive approaches to teaching and managing behaviour help to ensure that the child avoids too much failure and that self-esteem remains intact.
● Children whose appropriate learning and behaviour is noticed and

praised (using specific targeted praise rather than blanket praise) are more likely to repeat the behaviours which are attracting your admiration and to see themselves as helpful, clever and kind.

● Confidence and learning seem to be bound together. If a child tries something new and fails, their self-esteem and self-confidence becomes lower and they are less likely to try again.

Children who have epilepsy

Sometimes you might find yourself working with a child who not only has cognition and learning needs but also a medical condition as well. For example, a few children with cognition and learning needs might also have epilepsy and you will need to find out what this means for the child and what it means for you. Perhaps the cause of a child's learning difficulty was associated with a neurological difficulty early on that also caused the epilepsy, or perhaps severe epilepsy early in the child's life caused a degree of brain damage. Epileptic seizures or 'fits' are due to bursts of excessive electrical activity in the brain.

Seizures can take many forms and vary from child to child. The type of seizure depends on the part of the brain in which these bursts start and spread to. About one person in 200 is affected, with varying severity, and only a few will have learning difficulties as well. Medical investigations can often lead to medication that helps to control the epilepsy. These children have to be monitored by doctors as they grow older and their condition changes and, in fact, many children with epilepsy will grow out of it.

What you can do

● Talk to parents, carers or the school nurse to find out exactly what you should do in the event of a seizure. How will you recognise it and what happens?

● Make sure you know at what stage any emergency treatment should be called for, for example, if a seizure lasts two minutes longer than is usual for that child, or if the child begins to have another seizure before recovering from the first.

● If a child not known to have epilepsy throws a seizure, this would also be a case for calling an ambulance.

● If a child is having a seizure, protect them from injury by cushioning their head and placing the child on their side so that they can breathe easily. Do not restrict their movements or give them anything to drink. Stay with them until they have recovered.

● You will need to handle the seizure where it happens, so have a helper calmly reassure other children and draw them away to another activity, leaving you to await the recovery quietly and with privacy.

● If a child is having a partial seizure and is still conscious, lead them gently away from any danger and talk quietly to reassure them.

● For any medical condition, impending visits to hospital and clinics can be frightening until a child understands exactly what will happen. Talk with parents or carers if this is the case and use your regular learning activities and talking times to help.

Children with profound and multiple learning difficulties

Some children are profoundly disabled in all areas of their development and learning. They may have been described as having 'profound and multiple learning difficulties' (PMLD). Though most LEAs have special schools for children who need a high level of multi-disciplinary care and support, there are an increasing number of these children who are being included in local schools, particularly at Foundation Stage and Key Stage 1.

Perhaps their difficulties arose because of brain injury around birth or some other trauma. Perhaps something went wrong with their development very early in pregnancy, affecting the way in which their bodies and brains developed. Perhaps there is a chromosomal abnormality or other syndrome associated with profound developmental delay.

There can be enormous benefits from meeting the needs of these children in an inclusive primary school setting, so long as their difficulties have been carefully assessed, everybody works as a team, and the children can be supported appropriately. Usually, these children will have a statement of special educational needs from the LEA, describing their difficulties and the resources required to meet those needs.

What you can do

● The child is likely to have a learning support assistant allocated for their care. Try not to regard this person as 'the expert', but share the care and encouragement for the child across all colleagues so that you all learn and develop skills in meeting the child's multiple needs.

● Talk to parents or carers about how the child makes their needs known. How do they know when their child is tired, upset, hungry, or happy? Put together a communication book with photographs of the child and what their various expressions and behaviours mean. This can then be shared with all colleagues.

● You may need a quiet corner for the child if they are sleepy or need some peace.

● Look for activities where the child can feel and touch things and can enjoy interacting with others, at whatever level. Even if you are teaching something using words and pictures, find something that the child can explore on a sensory and tactile level.

● Refer to the early stages of the P scales to assist your target setting (see page 25) or contact a local special school for children with severe learning difficulties for outreach support or advice.

● Demonstrate to other children appropriate ways in which they can interact with the child and help them to 'tune in' with the child's responses.

● Find out which other professionals are involved so that you can share approaches and seek advice on 'next steps' to encourage. There is probably a local child development centre team involved or a team of therapists from the paediatric department of the local hospital.

Working with parents and carers

Parents often ask how they can help at home when the school expresses areas of concern. They might also approach you with their own concerns, which they need you to address with them. Parents have unique experience and expert knowledge of their own child, and you will need to create an ethos which shows how much this information is valued and made use of. Information sharing is important and is a two-way process. Here are some practical ways of involving parents in meeting their child's needs.

● Make a personal invitation to parents. For various reasons, parents do not always call into school on a daily basis. It is often helpful to invite parents into the class to share information about their child's achievements, in an informal way, or to arrange a home visit if possible.

● Draw the parents' attention to a specific display or specific examples of work, where examples of their child's progress can be seen and discussed.

● Invite the child to show what they can do or what has been learned for the parents to see.

● Ask parents for their opinions, by allowing opportunities for them to contribute information and share experiences. It is often helpful to set a regular time aside when other demands will not intrude.

● Thank parents and carers regularly for their support.

● Celebrate success with parents. This will ensure an ongoing positive partnership.

● Use a home–school diary to keep in touch.

The next step

If you think that a child in your setting has general learning difficulties, what does this mean for your practice? First of all, you will need to find a system of *assessment* that suits your particular situation. This is so that you can gather evidence of a child's strengths and weaknesses in order to plan suitable approaches. Assessment does not take place in a vacuum; it is an integral part of identifying need, planning for need, making an intervention and evaluating the outcome. You will read more about assessment in the next chapter and also in the *Special Needs Handbook* by Hannah Mortimer (Scholastic).

ASSESSING CHILDREN WITH COGNITIVE AND LEARNING DIFFICULTIES

Children with cognitive and learning difficulties require step-by-step approaches to help them make progress but also to 'learn how to learn'.

When does a child have SEN?

First, you need to remind yourself of the legal definition of SEN so that you can then apply this to your situation in order to decide whether or not the child with cognition and learning needs should be included within your SEN approaches. After all, you will be meeting a wide range of needs already in this area as part of your day-to-day classroom differentiation.

Children have SEN if they have a *learning difficulty* that calls for approaches which are *additional to* or *different from* usual. There is fuller information on how and when to decide that a child has SEN in the SEN *Code of Practice* and in the *Special Needs Handbook* by Hannah Mortimer (Scholastic) in this series.

There may be some children in your class where there has been no diagnosis of developmental, cognitive or learning difficulty as such but where you feel that their difficulties are causing barriers to their learning. When deciding whether or not a child has SEN, your informed judgement of whether these children are making adequate progress and whether you need to plan additional or different approaches is far more important than any outside diagnosis of a medical syndrome or developmental condition. Similarly, you cannot assume that because a child has a diagnosis you should place them on SEN approaches – the decision should be an individual one. If you are going to include these children in your SEN approaches, their difficulties have to be *significantly greater than for other children their age*. In other words, you are expected to be able to include a wide range of cognition and learning needs within your class as part of your everyday differentiation anyway. Usually, you will already be catering for the needs of children who are learning within two years either side of the average span of attainments for your year group.

What are the legal implications?

The SEN *Code of Practice* recommends that schools should identify children's needs and take action to meet those needs as early as possible, working with parents and carers. The aim is to enable all pupils with SEN to reach their full potential, to be included fully in their school communities and make a successful transition to adulthood. What are the underlying principles? All children have a right to a broad and balanced curriculum that enables them to make maximum progress. Teachers must recognise, identify and meet SEN within their school and plan a range of provision to meet those needs. Most children with SEN will be in a local mainstream school, even those who have statements of SEN. Parents, children, schools

and support services should work as partners in planning for and meeting SEN.

It is acknowledged that good practice can take many forms and teachers are encouraged to adopt a flexible and a graduated response to the SEN of individual children. This approach recognises that there is a continuum of SEN and, where necessary, brings increasing specialist expertise on board if the child is experiencing continuing difficulties. Once a child's SEN have been identified, school staff should intervene through School Action and plan an individual education plan (IEP).

When reviewing the child's progress and the help they are receiving, you might decide to seek alternative approaches to learning with the aid of outside support services. These interventions are known as School Action Plus. This phase is characterised by the involvement of specialists from outside the school. The SENCO now takes a leading role, working closely with the member of staff responsible for the child, and:

● draws on advice from outside specialists, for example, support teachers or educational psychologists

● makes sure that the child and parents are consulted and kept informed

● ensures that an IEP is still drawn up (usually by the class teacher) incorporating the specialist advice, and that it is incorporated within the curriculum planning for the whole school

● makes certain that the child's progress is reviewed with outside specialists and parents and carers

● keeps the headteacher informed.

For a very small number of children, the help provided by School Action Plus will still not be sufficient to ensure satisfactory progress, even when it has run over several review periods. The provider,

external professionals and parents may then decide to ask the LEA to consider carrying out a statutory assessment of the child's SEN. The LEA must decide quickly whether or not it has the evidence to indicate that a statutory assessment is necessary for a child. It is then responsible for coordinating a statutory assessment and will call for the various reports that it requires, from the teacher, an educational psychologist, a doctor (who will also gather evidence from any speech and language therapist involved), and the social services department if involved, and will ask parents to submit their own views. Once it has collected in the evidence, the LEA might decide to issue a statement of SEN for the child. Only children with severe and long-standing SEN who need a high level of additional support go on to receive a statement – about two per cent of children. There are various rights of appeal in cases of disagreement, and the LEA can provide information about these.

What do I do now?

You are likely to find yourself in one of two situations. Perhaps there is a child moving into your class who has already been identified as having SEN linked to their cognition or learning needs. Your way forward is clear. You should proceed to monitor the SEN and set a regular individual education plan (IEP), either as part of School Action, School Action Plus or as part of any statemented provision that has been set by the LEA. If the system is working as it should be, there should be information and programmes already available from the previous school or class. This should give you enough to plan your interventions and you will need to carry out a fuller assessment before the next IEP review so that you can advise on whether additional and different approaches are still required. Once in a certain phase of the SEN approaches (for example, School Action or School Action Plus), it does not mean that a child is destined to remain there. Movement between the different phases should depend on the needs of the child, present progress and current barriers to learning.

In the second scenario, you yourself might have concerns about a child's cognition and learning needs and progress. Perhaps you are identifying a child's SEN for the first time. Here, you need to carry out a thorough assessment in order to identify what aspects of the pupil's learning require additional or different approaches. You will find some basic advice below and the school's SENCO will help you decide whether the results of your assessment suggest SEN approaches.

Including all children

The DfES has produced guidelines on how to include all children in the Literacy Hour and Daily Mathematics Lesson and thus make the National Literacy and Numeracy Strategies (NLS and NNS) more accessible (details on pages 95 to 96). These are especially relevant for children who have cognition and learning needs and there will be copies in your school held by the headteacher, SENCO, literacy and mathematics coordinators. The guidelines have detailed

information about how to plan provision in literacy and mathematics for children who have SEN, how to choose appropriate learning objectives, how to plan strategies for enabling children with different learning styles to access the curriculum and how to see all of this through into planning units of work in the Literacy Hour and Daily Mathematics Lesson. The 'graduated response' recommended in the SEN *Code of Practice* can be broadly mapped on to the NLS/NNS Three-wave Framework in this way:

Wave One: the effective inclusion of all the children in a quality Daily Mathematics Lesson and Literacy Hour

Wave Two: small group interventions for children who should be expected to 'catch up' with their peers, given this extra support

Wave Three: additional and different approaches under the SEN *Code of Practice.*

In Wave Three, you might feel that it is not in a child's best interests to work on the same activities and objectives as the class as a whole. These are the children who have SEN and for whom you might need to 'track back' to a more elementary programme of objectives, either at an earlier level of the National Curriculum or on to the QCA P scales, which describe children's achievements at each of eight pre-National Curriculum levels. The *Including All Children in the Literacy Hour and Daily Mathematics Lesson* document gives you guidance for tracking back through the Frameworks and, as such, should be an essential read for all teachers. The SENCO should be able to support colleagues through this approach.

You will find the two-week planning sheets particularly helpful since they enable you to visualise 'real' children and 'real' needs in a classroom context, with practical suggestions for progression and also what to do if the suggestions do not work. For those of us who learn by visualising and doing, as well as by reading, these kinds of example are invaluable and will help you to see that you already have many special skills to call on when planning for children with SEN.

The individual education plan

Individual education plans (IEPs) should be a key feature of planning for any SEN in your school, either as part of your School Action or your School Action Plus. They should contain three or four short-term targets and make it clear how you will know that your teaching has been successful. The IEP should lead to the child making progress and should be seen as an integrated aspect of the curriculum planning for the whole class.

You should be differentiating the curriculum for a range of individual needs anyway, and so an IEP need only include that which is additional to or different from the regular curriculum that is in place for all the children. When children have common targets (and common teaching strategies) in a class, it is possible for you to write a Group Education Plan.

There is no set format, and you need to design an IEP which is clear, accessible and understandable for your school. The SENCO will advise you on the best format to use and there is further information

in the *Special Needs Handbook* by Hannah Mortimer (Scholastic), also in this series. You might include:

- the name of the child
- whether you are planning School Action or School Action Plus
- the nature of the child's difficulty
- a list of the child's strengths
- the action you are planning
- who will do what
- the help that will come from parents or carers
- three or four targets for the term
- your monitoring and assessment arrangements
- when you will review the IEP with parents
- who else you will invite to the review meeting.

Targets should be 'SMART'– specific, measurable, achievable, realistic and time bound, for example: 'By the end of this term, Philip will be able to write a short sentence of independent writing, coming to me for difficult spellings.'

The IEP should underpin all your planning and intervention for the child with cognition and learning needs and should therefore be shared with colleagues, parents and carers. It must include what should be taught, how it should be taught and how often the additional or different provision will be made. You can also use the IEP to show how you will differentiate (break down) your activities in order to make the curriculum accessible to those children who have SEN. Some schools make use of the P scales when planning individual targets for children with cognition and learning needs.

The P scales

The document *Supporting the Target Setting Process* (DfEE/QCA 2001) provides guidance for schools to help them plan effective targets for children with SEN, particularly if children are not yet working at the level of National Curriculum. Performance criteria (or P scales) are given to describe children's attainment leading to Level 1 and within Levels 1 and 2 of certain strands of the National Curriculum. These have been written for use with children of all ages and with a wide range of SEN and are particularly useful for those with cognition and learning needs. P scales do not describe everything the child learns; neither do they replace any more finely tuned assessments you might choose to make. However, they are a useful framework on which to hang progress and enable you to track back to earlier stages of learning.

Some LEAs have published methods of performance monitoring and effective target setting that track through from P Scales to higher levels of the National Curriculum. The 'PIVATS' approach is published by Lancashire County Council and it is possible to subscribe to the PIVATS website for franchise agreements, updates and data. You will find contact details on pages 95 to 96. PIVATS tracks progress as far as Level 4 of the National Curriculum, breaking down learning targets into easier steps for the strands of English, Mathematics, Science and Personal, social and emotional development.

How can I get support?

Schools have always had their own funding to support children who are not making adequate progress. Sometimes teachers or parents worry that children will only have access to additional funding if they are receiving School Action Plus or if they have a statement of SEN. Nowadays, most of the SEN budget is delegated to schools and clusters, and each school has a ring-fenced amount for supporting children's progress where necessary. However, each school will choose to use its funding in a particular way and to target additional support where it feels it is most needed. Some schools find it most successful to target funding for teaching assistants attached to particular age groups or classes.

Where you have Wave Two intervention programmes, you might have any of a range of additional adults working with the children – SEN support teachers (from the school, cluster or LEA), teaching assistants, ethnic minority achievement (EMA) teachers, learning mentors, trainee teachers and voluntary helpers. These people need to feel clear about their roles and also have knowledge of the curriculum offered to the whole group. Again, there are full guidelines in the *Including All Children in the Literacy Hour and Daily Mathematics Lesson* document. Wave Three intervention is specifically targeted at children identified as requiring SEN support. Sometimes this involves a learning support assistant working with a named child or group of children.

These pointers will help you use this support most effectively for the child. Do discuss them with any support assistant you are working with – it is very helpful for them to realise that 'support' need not mean 'shadowing'.

● Remember that the purpose of inclusion is not for a child to spend the full school day with grown-ups! Never underestimate what children can learn from each other, particularly if friendship groups are encouraged.

● A child will never feel part of a class, school or community if they are isolated in a separate room or area with a support assistant or specialist tutor. However, if withdrawal is felt to be needed, then involve other children too, perhaps creating a small withdrawal group.

● The purpose of the supporter is not to 'hover over', 'shadow' or 'stick like glue' but to be aware of the child's individual targets and needs and to facilitate their inclusion and their progress.

● The art of support is to find the balance between teaching and developing the child's initiative. Over-use of support can lead to children not doing anything until they are prompted.

● Effective support will usually be aimed at enabling the child to participate in a group rather than the provision of one-to-one attention.

● Sometimes this means breaking steps down so that a child can access a particular activity. The photocopiable planning sheet on page 31 will help you do this.

● At other times, effective support involves modifying the activity or lesson to include the child.

The Disability Act

The Disability Discrimination Act (DDA) 1995 brought in new legal measures to clarify disabled people's rights in terms of employment, obtaining goods and services, buying or renting land or property and transport. The Act was amended to cover the requirements on establishments which provide education for children and this formed the Special Educational Need and Disability Act (SENDA) 2001.

● Under the Act, a disabled person has 'a physical or mental impairment, which has an effect on his or her ability to carry out normal day-to-day activities. That effect must be substantial (not trivial or minor), adverse and long-term'.

● Schools are also required to overcome physical features which impede access to a service. They will have to make 'reasonable adjustments' to the physical environment to overcome physical barriers to access both for pupils and for disabled adults.

● You cannot refuse a service (such as education), offer a worse standard of service or offer a service on worse terms to a disabled child or person unless you can offer a 'justification'. This is called the 'less favourable treatment' duty. Even so, you will be expected to demonstrate that you are planning ahead to improve access and inclusion in the future.

● You need to plan 'reasonable adjustments' for disabled children. This might include training for personal support assistants, planning accessible activities in an accessible environment, flexibility in terms of toilet arrangements and the provision of flexible transport.

● Plan school outings well ahead so that children with disabilities can be included. If you are short of staff on an outing, it would probably be seen as a 'reasonable adjustment' to invite a parent or carer to come too in order to help.

● Make sure that children who cannot walk or stand are not left out – organise an alternative activity that is at floor level and includes all the children.

● Plan ways of including all the children in group and circle time. If a child is non-verbal, look for alternative ways they can join in, answer the register and so on.

● Teach staff members some basic sign language and share this with all the children.

● Always keep records that explain why you are making adjustments and how you are monitoring their effectiveness.

Learning to learn

It is one thing to be able to break down curriculum areas into finer steps and to track back until the child's present progress is represented. It is another thing to look more closely at how a child with cognition needs is actually learning so that you can teach them step by small step to learn more effectively. For example, children with cognition needs usually have difficulties in their attention and memory systems and they may have very particular learning styles. Whenever we learn anything new, we need to:

● focus our attention

● look/listen/feel the information (linked to 'learning style')

- hold it in our short-term or working memories long enough to make sense of it
- build it into our long-term memories
- generalise it to different situations
- retrieve it at the right time.

By looking at ways of assessing attention, learning style and memory, it is possible to gain a better understanding of how a child with cognitive difficulties is functioning. This can then be used to provide more effective support as the child 'learns how to learn'.

Assessing attention

Here is a checklist for assessing attention very broadly arranged in developmental stages, though there are always individual differences. Use this list to develop your own form and put a tick box after each statement to check each stage the child has reached. Then break down the next stages step by small step, setting specific targets to enable the child to improve attention skills.

Assessing attention

Does the child:

Free choice

- Use a trial and error approach when playing with toys and equipment?
- Attend very differently depending on the activity?
- Switch attention easily by flitting from one activity to another?
- Become absorbed in their own choice of activity?
- Pay attention to a chosen activity but is easily distracted from it?
- Listen and respond to others in a social way while attending to an activity?
- Select, plan and review a play or learning activity with intermittent support?

General

- Anticipate a familiar routine?
- Make their basic needs known to an interested adult?
- Follow a picture timetable of what comes next with one-to-one support?
- Respond to their name across a room?
- Attend to and respond to simple class rules?
- Listen to the speaker at group time for a few minutes?
- Follow a simple group instruction?

Directed activity

- Sustain attention on a short set activity with one-to-one support?
- Stop an activity and listen to the teacher with one-to-one support?
- Listen to class instruction when focused by name first?
- Attend to a short enjoyable task working with a partner?
- Attend to a short set task in a small group with group adult support?
- Attend to a short set task in a large group with group adult support?

Writing

- Attend to a short piece of written work with one-to-one support?
- Attend to a short piece of written work in a distraction-free work area with intermittent support?
- Attend to a short piece of written work in a distraction-free work area and come to seek support when needed?
- Complete a short piece of written work independently working alongside others?
- Work in a small group involving a written task with intermittent support?
- Work in a large class group with intermittent support?

Keep activities motivating

You will find that you can train attention best by keeping activities especially motivating. The photocopiable sheet on page 32 is just one way of designing reward charts to support a child's learning.

Assessing learning styles

When designing your teaching approaches for children with cognition and learning needs, it makes sense to assess what kind of learners they are. We all learn by looking, listening or doing, and some of us are better than others at learning visually, auditorily or kinaesthetically. Just as children who are cognitively very able are usually successful in all three learning styles, children who have cognitive difficulties are usually challenged in one or several styles of learning. Some, you will find, are very strong when learning in one medium. For example, those who have autistic spectrum difficulties are usually most successful when presented with visual information. Children with attention deficit with hyperactivity can be very practical thinkers and prefer to learn kinaesthetically. Other children might have more general difficulties and need your support across all their learning. This is why you will find that activities that appeal to all three learning styles and are presented in a multi-sensory way are most successful when including children with cognitive difficulties. If you suspect a real weakness in visual or auditory learning, remember to make sure that vision and hearing are unimpaired.

The checklist on photocopiable page 30 is an example of how you can use focused observation and discussion with the children themselves to narrow down on their most successful learning style. Photocopy the form and simply circle the letter if a statement seems to apply and see whether one style is more prevalent than any other.

Working with memory difficulties

A qualitative assessment of memory skills will help you assess particular areas of weakness. You can usually work out whether a child best remembers information that is seen, heard or handled by setting up learning activities and assessing this on an ongoing basis. For children with learning needs, it is not sufficient simply to teach them something new. As a teacher, you will find that you have to provide that learning in a repetitive way, looking for new and interesting methods of helping the child consolidate and generalise the information learned. You can use a variety of ways of supporting memory – aim to help the child to recognise information before you expect them to retrieve it from their memories 'cold'. You can:
- offer multiple choice
- prompt recall with a picture or prop
- provide the first sound of the word to be remembered
- focus them in with the context
- keep and reuse digital photographs of an earlier learning situation in order to prompt recall of the objective learned
- 'prime the pump' by working through an exercise with them first
- provide audio tapes of directions.

Assessment of learning styles

Name _____ Year group _____

Reading
● When presented with an illustrated book, does the child enjoy looking through the pictures? **V**
● Does the child enjoy listening to stories rather than reading them? **A**
● Does the child enjoy reading books? **V**
● Is the child good at explaining stories? **A**
● Does the child prefer listening to story tapes? **A**
● Does close print confuse the child? **A**
● Does the child fiddle a lot when reading? **K**
● Is the child good at using expression and tone of voice? **A**

Writing
● Has the child developed reasonable handwriting? **K**
● Does the child tend to think out loud when writing? **A**
● Does the child enjoy writing in their own words? **K**
● Does the child embellish text with illustrations, diagrams and decoration? **V & K**
● Does the child spell best by saying the letter sounds out loud? **A**
● Does the child spell best when actually writing text and then checking? **V**
● Does the child enjoy working in diagrams, mind maps and pictures? **K**

Mathematics
● Does the child need to work through examples with your support first in order to grasp a new concept? **K**

● Can the child learn by simply watching you work an example through first? **V**
● Does the child talk themselves through examples out loud? **A**
● Can the child follow your spoken instructions? **A**
● Does the child prefer concrete counters and aids to number? **K**

General
● Does the child enjoy music making? **A**
● Does the child like to watch others first before joining in with anything new? **V**
● Does the child need instructions repeated? **V**
● Does the child gesticulate when speaking? **K**
● Has the child had speech and language difficulties? **V**
● Would the child rather demonstrate something than explain it? **K**
● Does the child need to look directly at the speaker in order to understand better? **K**
● Does the child have difficulty remembering unless a note is made? **V & A**
● Does the child daydream a lot during listening activities? **V**
● Does the child prefer to watch an activity rather than 'get stuck in'? **V**
● Does the child enjoy art and craft? **V & K**
● Is the child a real 'doer'? **K**
● Is the child easily distracted by noise? **A**

Summary of learning style
A – auditory: .... out of 12
V – visual: .... out of 12
K – kinaesthetic or tactile: .... out of 12

Step-by-step planning sheet

Name _____ **Year group** _____

Use this sheet to break targets down into smaller, more manageable steps.

Present ability _____

_____

Step	Short-term target	Date achieved
1		
2		
3		
4		
5		
6		

Long-term target _____

_____

Name _____ **Year group** _____

I've been a BUSY BEE

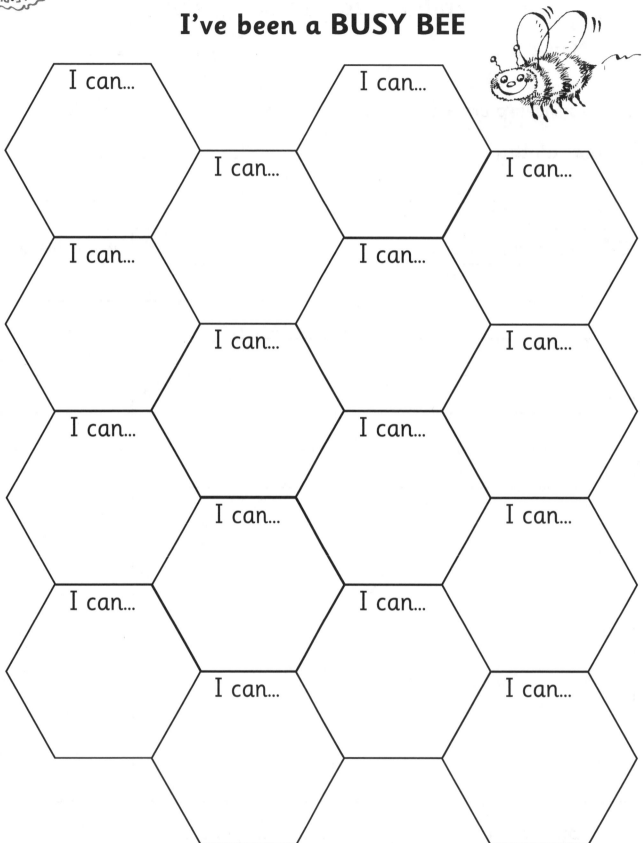

I can...

I can...

I can...

I can...

I can...

I can...

I can...

I can...

I can...

I can...

I can...

I can...

I can...

I can...

Celebrate each new achievement by writing it on the honeycomb.

PLANNING INTERVENTIONS

This chapter provides you with a tool bag of approaches for supporting children with cognitive and learning difficulties.

Once you have assessed a child's pattern of strengths and weaknesses, thereby establishing the starting point for your teaching, how can you differentiate your teaching so that each step will be achievable by the child who has learning difficulties? All of the approaches to differentiation below are common sense and arise from your personal knowledge and experience of the child and their needs. Taking time in the early stages to closely observe and monitor the child can help 'tune in' to the way in which children are experiencing the lesson and allow for more practical differentiation where opportunities are lacking.

Once you have decided where you are starting from in your teaching (assessment) and planned a differentiated teaching approach (intervention), then you will need to carefully monitor the child's progress and share this with parents, continually reviewing how you are all doing and where to go next. You will find more ideas about this in the *Special Needs Handbook* by Hannah Mortimer (Scholastic). The approaches described in this chapter appear in italic in the support sections of each activity, allowing you to cross-reference the ideas more easily.

Working with strengths

Adjust the response

Some children may be able to show they have learned through actions rather than words and any response that the child is able to give needs to be valued. Some children, for example, may rely on sign language, while others may not be able to tell you their wishes but can demonstrate by their smiles, their choices or their behaviour where they would like to work.

Alternative means of recording

You will find a helpful pull-out sheet at the back of the NLS and NNS publication *Including All Children in the Literacy Hour and Daily Mathematics Lesson*. For children who find it hard to record their ideas in writing, consider asking them to create displays or posters, make digital photo spreads, create mind maps or flow charts, or present their work on video or tape. Sometimes a child with learning needs may be able to work with a partner who can scribe for them while they dictate. Sometimes multiple-choice answers (not necessarily in word form) can be highlighted or labels matched to texts and pictures.

Appropriate content

The content of the story or discussion session, for example, may need to be at a level appropriate to the child's stage of language. Even if you are addressing the whole group, you might need to include concrete props to hold an individual child's attention, emphasise meaning and allow that child to participate with more than one sense.

Assess learning style

Spend time working out whether the child learns best by looking, listening or doing – in other words whether they are primarily visual, auditory or kinaesthetic learners or a combination of these. You will find further information and a possible approach on page 30.

Clear expectations

As with all children, those with cognition and learning needs can respond totally differently in different classrooms because the expectations on them are different. If you expect a child not to learn, then that is what you are likely to experience. If you know that a child can learn given time and opportunity, then present your teaching at the right level for the child to succeed. Break steps down, slow the pace down and pause to give the child time to respond to show that a successful outcome is clearly expected.

Give feedback

Children with cognition and learning needs require regular feedback on how they are learning. Target your feedback directly to the child and make it specific and positive by using clear, observable language, for example: 'Yes – sentences begin with capital letters – well done!'

Special responsibilities

Children with cognition and learning needs often lack self-esteem and it is very helpful to give them particular school or class responsibilities in order to develop their self-worth. Special responsibilities give the child very appropriate prestige in front of the other children and can assist inclusion.

Teach reading to improve language

Research conducted by the Sarah Duffen Centre states that children with Down's syndrome benefit from being taught to read early and that this also brings on their language skills. The research findings suggest that these children are primarily visual learners and can often learn to read well, with spelling, phonetic skills, language and understanding following on behind. Contact the centre at www.downsed.org for details of research, approaches and resources.

Use ICT

Computers are an effective means of learning and recording for pupils with cognition and learning needs since they are intrinsically rewarding and provide opportunities for repetitive learning and

consolidation. They also allow children to present their written work in a pleasing format that they can feel proud of.

Working with weaknesses

Adult support
Some children need more individual adult support and time. This can include some one-to-one work or withdrawal into a small group, but mainly refers to supporting the child with additional encouragement and prompting within the regular group. Simply having a heightened awareness of the child's individual needs can affect teacher involvement. In an inclusive setting, any time spent relating individually to an adult would take place in the classroom itself, with opportunities for involving other children as well.

Altering the pace
Allow the child extra time to respond, or ensure that they sometimes have opportunities to 'get there first'. These are ways of building up their confidence. Activities may need to be presented at a slower pace to ensure understanding or a succession of materials presented to maintain interest during a discussion. Some children need to 'sandwich' short periods of structured activity with periods of free play or quiet. Some children take a long time to process information, and need longer silences than usual if they are to answer a question or fulfil a request. Others may find it hard to remember more than the last piece of information given them and therefore need support and prompting at each step, taking longer to carry out structured activities.

Being patient
You may need to wait longer than usual before a child responds to what you have asked for. Give a child with cognition and learning needs time to respond before you come in with a repetition or the answer. Sometimes these children need longer than usual to process what you have just said or shown them before they can then put together their response. Sometimes simple signing is used in order to make instructions and requests clearer.

Break steps down
Let the pupil sit where you can provide help unobtrusively. Break down written tasks into smaller steps and help the child organise work before it is begun. A small amount of individual attention from you before work is started can save a great deal of recovery work later. You can break steps down by grading the amount of help you provide, changing the level of the task, altering the amount you expect or using simpler materials.

Communication book
Provide plenty of encouragement whenever the child communicates with you, whether they have done so with their voice or their actions. For children with delayed verbal skills, you might need to

put together a communication book to help other adults and children in your school understand how a child communicates. You might start with:

This is how Jack shows us he is interested…

This is how Amie shows us she is anxious…

This is how Geri shows us she is bored…

This is how Ashish shows us he needs time in the quiet corner…

Engaging attention

Children with cognition and learning needs often have poor attention skills and are easily distracted. Use their names clearly, get down to their level, encourage eye contact and then speak. When you are issuing instructions to the whole class, address the child with attention difficulties by name first to engage attention. Give very clear and simple messages, showing the child what to do as well as telling. You may need to set up distraction-free areas for work, depending on whether a child is more likely to be distracted by fiddling, sights or sounds.

Keep it concrete

Children with cognition and learning needs are more likely to need concrete materials to handle and calculate with and props for imaginative work. Children at earlier stages of their development will still find it easiest to learn by involving their senses and by linking actions with their learning.

Motivators

One of the challenges in teaching young children with cognition and learning needs is that they might require stronger than usual motivators if they are to learn. If you decide to use stickers or tokens, always pair these with social praise so that, in time, the child comes to see the praise as rewarding as well. You can also make sure the work itself is intrinsically motivating for a child with cognition and learning needs by ensuring that there is always an element of success.

Learning mentors

Pair a member of staff with a child who has cognition and learning needs and arrange for them to meet together so that the adult can help the child monitor their own progress, sharing helpful advice along the way. Some schools recruit specially selected and vetted learning mentors from outside the school environment.

Personal best

Some children may feel that they can never compare to others and success might feel a long way off for them, or even impossible. Expect their *personal best* rather than a total improvement. Help children with cognition and learning needs set their own *personal best* targets and monitor how they feel they are doing.

Shaping

When you are moving towards a particularly desirable skill for a child (such as written letter formation), you cannot expect to get there straight away. Start by accepting even a tiny approximation to that desired skill (for example, holding the pencil correctly) and praising it. This is called *shaping* and many behaviours and learning targets lend themselves to this kind of approach.

Using a key worker

Start by helping the child feel settled when learning in a small group with a familiar and supportive adult or key worker. In practice, this is often a learning support assistant allocated to a child with cognition and learning needs. For younger children, that worker can begin by simply working or playing in parallel to the child, gently leading the child on and extending their knowledge, understanding and skills.

Working with opportunities

Access

This involves both the way in which you remove physical barriers to learning and the way in which materials and resources are presented. Some children may need adapted scissors to cut out a picture or require photographs rather than line drawings in order to make sense of visual information. Pictures and illustrations might need to be simplified to cut down on additional and confusing information.

Choices

Offer a child with a language delay choices or alternatives when being asked a question (such as: 'Do you want to finish your story or work on your model?'). Illustrations and concrete props can help the development of vocabulary.

Circle time

The process of *circle time* involves key skills required of any individual belonging to a social group: awareness (knowing who I am), mastery (knowing what I can do) and social interaction (knowing

how I function in the world of others). This is an effective approach for including and supporting all kinds of SEN. You can also use circles to deliver the National Curriculum when you are working in groups.

Extend imagination

Look for opportunities to help the child think and play imaginatively and to develop symbolic skills. This is especially helpful if the child can learn to play imaginatively with another child, providing opportunities for developing their own imaginative ideas and language. Encourage imaginative thinking and pretend play by basing this on 'real life' experiences at first. You might act out going to a party together or visiting the supermarket. Miniature play and re-enactments, such as with small-world resources, can also be helpful and will mean that other children enjoy the learning situation as well.

Grouping

The group structure may afford opportunities to allow the child to respond or for other members of the group to provide good models which can reinforce the child's learning. Sometimes meeting the needs of individual children with learning difficulties has led to children working alone with individual materials. This is not providing the child with an inclusive curriculum. Arrangements to include the child's individual education plan within planning for the *whole group* can overcome this and lead to a more purposeful and supportive way of meeting special needs.

Mind mapping

Mind mapping is a very important technique for improving the way children take notes. By using mind maps, you show the structure of the subject and links between points, as well as the raw facts contained in normal notes. Mind maps hold information in a format that the mind finds easy to remember and quick to review.

Non-verbal modelling

Children can be shown (as well as told) how to sort the concept blocks, organise the puppets for a play, gather data for an experiment. Children with global delay sometimes also have difficulties in fine-motor coordination and you may need to show the child how to use a pencil or paintbrush, how to enjoy writing and artwork, and even how to become more personally independent.

Peer support

Pair older and younger children together and arrange for them to meet to practise reading or mathematics. You will need to spend time with the 'mentors' showing them what to do and monitor the progress carefully. Some schools have found this kind of regular peer support very beneficial for the older and younger children alike. In fact, with your support and supervision, it can sometimes be very

helpful for an older pupil with learning difficulties to mentor a younger child in early reading skills.

Positive affirmations

A whole class can do this! Rehearsing together positive affirmations (for example, 'I can do this' or, 'I am good at reading') can actually help to fulfil the prophecy. Practise saying to a mirror in the morning, 'I *can* support all the cognition and learning needs in my class!'

Play power

You may find that some children apply their learning most confidently during play and free-activity times. Try to build these sessions into the regular day. Look for occasions when you can use language and learning together in a non-direct way, perhaps by talking easily and informally while the child is involved in a creative activity. Build on the fact that children with significant cognition and learning needs may still be at a stage where they need sensory experiences. You can also use a free-play area for children to unwind between more challenging activities.

Self-esteem building

There are certain approaches that you can use in order to promote high self-esteem and confidence in all the children. Plan *circle-time* activities, appoint a *key worker* for vulnerable children, work in smaller groups to help a child feel less socially 'overloaded' and more secure, plan learning activities which allow you to talk about feelings and offer children choices in their learning and activities whenever appropriate. Use positive behavioural approaches, praise and encouragement to prompt more appropriate attitudes to learning.

Sequence

Some children need to have opportunities provided at different times, or need to cover different aspects of a topic at separate sessions. If attention is short, it might be necessary to revisit an activity at another time in order to ensure success. Some children find it harder to settle and to concentrate after they have been very active. Others need to 'let off steam' for a while in order to return more attentively to an activity.

Small-group tuition

Talk to the SENCO if you feel that small-group or individual tuition is necessary. Most LEAs have now delegated learning support to local school clusters and you should find out what level of support is available in your area. Sometimes support teachers come in to advise class teachers on their approaches. At other times, the support teacher or SENCO will take a small group for specialist literacy teaching. In other schools still, pupils might be withdrawn to attend special units or tutorials at dyslexia centres. Creative use of classroom assistance (when available!) or parent help can sometimes release *you* to spend time with a small group of children.

Starting points

When a child first starts school, you need to get to know the child well and to have a clear starting point for your support. Talk with parents and carers. Find out about how much the child understands and how well they can express themselves. How do they make their needs known? Ask parents to tape some language or video some play at home (where the child is most relaxed), so that you can have a 'feel' of their stage even if the child says very little in school. Plan transfers between classes carefully so that you can build on each other's information and experience – both formally (your documentation) and informally (how well you each know the child).

Support planning and persistence

Take time to support children in planning what they are going to do next, and help them to see this through and evaluate how it has gone and what they think about it. Spend time at the beginning of an activity talking about what you are going to do together and how. For example, if you are about to make a poster together, talk about what it will show and who it will be for. Focus on how you will make it. Then focus on how you will display it.

Using the right language

Language needs to be clear and positive and at the right level for a child to understand. Engage attention first, emphasise key words and keep sentences short and simple. For example, '*Mohammed – one* finger space between each word – like *this*.'

Working with challenges

Chaining

Sometimes you can break a complex social skill down and teach it step by step, eventually stringing the skills together. This is called *chaining*, because it is similar to making each link in a chain and then chaining all the links together. For example, you might teach an inattentive pupil to ask for help when stuck, by targeting and praising this behaviour. You might then teach them to work independently at a task for five minutes at a side table. Then they could learn to finish one task and move on to another. Eventually

you can string these skills together by setting more complex targets, thereby encouraging that child to work independently.

Checking level

When you are planning how to deliver the curriculum to your class, you are bound to be making allowances for different levels of children's ability. Within this, it might be that some children need the learning steps broken down more finely (using *task analysis*), and it may be necessary to give value to a smaller and less obvious learning outcome.

Individualise texts

Provide enlarged and simplified photocopies of any worksheets that carry a lot of dense text or reprint them with double spacing – this makes them easier to scan and to focus upon. If pupils have a lot of written copying to be done in a lesson, provide a more visual or simplified version for a pupil with cognition or learning needs to keep instead.

Improving memory skills

Memory games can be usefully done at home if there is not the time in school. There are some simple ideas in the boxed section.

Memory games to play at home

I spy

Start with three or four items on a tray and say, for example: 'I spy with my little eye something beginning with *t*.' Gradually build up the number of items. Move on to 'I spy with my little eye something ending with *t*.' Later, try 'I spy' on long car journeys.

Kim's game

Place three or four items on a tray. Ask your child to look at them for ten seconds. Secretly remove one. Which is missing? Gradually build up the quantity.

Dice games

Any! Your child needs to make quick visual judgements based on the pattern of the spots, without the need to count them out. 'Snakes and ladders', 'Beetle' and 'Ludo' are all starting points.

Reversals

Make some playing cards out of common reversals such as b/d/p/q. Make it clear where the bottom of the letter is by drawing in a line for the letter to sit on. Use them to play 'Snap'. Adapt them to play 'Lotto' or 'Bingo'. Use them to play 'Pairs'.

Mnemonics

Involve the child in working out useful mnemonics for remembering particularly difficult spellings (for example, 'Big elephants can always understand small elephants – b.e.c.a.u.s.e'). Make a picture of your favourite mnemonics so that visual learners remember them too. Collect rhymes and verses that aid spelling rules (such as, '*i* before *e* except after *c*'). Try setting them to a rap or to music to aid remembering.

SMC teaching: Structured, Multi-sensory and Cumulative

This is a simple step-by-step approach that is:
● structured – follows all the skills that have to be acquired in a logical and comprehensive way
● multi-sensory – uses every sense so that different connections are strengthened in the brain, weaknesses are compensated for and fluency and recall improved
● cumulative – allows each skill to build on the one before so that confidence and attainments build progressively.
You can make use of commercially available support programmes (see catalogue suppliers on pages 95 to 96) or adapt your own based on the NLS and NNS *Including All Children in the Literacy Hour and Daily Mathematics Lesson* publication.

Structure

Some children learn best when they are playing in a highly structured setting, led and supported by an adult. Others seem to respond best when provided with free exploration and are supported in developing their own agendas. Every child needs opportunities to learn both on their own terms and in groups with other adults and children.

Task analysis

Task analysis refers to the breaking down of an individual teaching target into several smaller steps or component skills. You then plan the order in which you will teach the steps, starting with the step that will come easiest to the child and finishing with the most

challenging step for that particular child and their set of needs. There are many different ways in which you can make step sizes smaller. One of the most common techniques is to introduce different ways of prompting and helping the child reach the target using verbal, physical or visual prompting. The selection of appropriate prompts depends on the child's current skill level. As a rule you should write into a programme only enough aid to help the child reach the targeted behaviour. In successive weeks you should aim to demonstrate progress, step by small step.

SPEAKING AND LISTENING

Language pervades so much of what we do and no more so than in school. Children who have cognition and learning needs will often have been slower than their peers to develop spoken language and understanding, and it could be that their poor language skills are still creating a real barrier to their learning. Sometimes these barriers can be quite subtle – perhaps a child only remembers part of what you say, only follows very simple instructions or does not understand abstract or complex spoken information, even if that child's technical reading skills are fine. The speaking and listening strand of the National Curriculum can provide you with opportunities for assessing how a child's language skills are progressing making it possible for you to *check level*. Sometimes the results of your assessment can come as a surprise – you might find that a child who appeared to be coping fine with the social language demands of day-to-day interaction really struggles when it comes to thinking, reasoning, predicting and remembering using more complex language.

Altering the pace of a speaking and listening activity and *being patient* can allow a child with cognition and learning needs to process the information and respond. Make sure you *use the right language* for the child to be able to process and *support planning and persistence* by teaching and encouraging appropriate looking and listening skills. *Keep it concrete* by providing props and illustrations, 'priming' the child ahead of an activity by introducing the topic, new vocabulary and concepts through *small-group tuition*. *Engage attention* during discussion work by using name and eye contact, reframing the question to avoid complex or abstract language. *Circle time* provides excellent opportunities for speaking and listening, and allows children with cognition and learning needs to learn from their friends and to develop attention and memory skills.

When you *assess learning styles*, you will probably find that some children with cognition and learning needs are comparatively strong visual or kinaesthetic learners. These children will particularly benefit from speaking and listening time. Other children may find that reading is an easier area and you can sometimes *teach reading to improve language* and use *individualised texts* to develop their speaking and listening skills. For example, when participating in group talking tasks, children can prepare and read from their own text if they have thought about the topic in advance. Throughout the activity chapters that follow, you will find that phrases in italic can be cross-referenced to the interventions in Chapter 3 for a fuller explanation.

AGE RANGE
Five to seven.

GROUP SIZE
Whole class, in pairs and small groups.

LEARNING OBJECTIVE FOR ALL THE CHILDREN
● To listen and follow instructions accurately.

INDIVIDUAL LEARNING TARGET
● To look at the teacher, listen and respond to group instructions.

Story time

Children with cognition and learning needs may need to be taught how to listen and respond in a large group.

What you need
Prepared instructions (such as, *cross your arms*; *sit down*); a short story; listening boards (A4 paper divided into four); photocopiable page 50 (Section B enlarged); coloured cubes (optional).

Preparation
Cut out and display the speaking parts from Section B of photocopiable page 50.

What to do
Use the two listening exercises below to warm up the class, before beginning the main activity.

Susie says
Play this version of 'Simon says' to focus listening attention. Give the children a series of instructions. When you forget to say *Susie says*, the children should respond, 'No!'

Draw a story
Give out the listening boards. Read the children a short story, divided into four manageable 'chunks'. Pause after the first part for talk partners to confer on events and draw that chunk of the story in the first box of the listening board. Repeat for the remaining parts. Ask the children to retell the story to each other from their drawings.

Story time
You are going to read a story together, but only you will have the whole story. Divide the class into the necessary number of groups.

Display and assign spoken parts from section B of the photocopiable sheet. Emphasise that groups must *listen* carefully and *look* at you in order to know when to speak. Try colour-coding words and groups – a red cube held next to your face could mean that the red group has to say the red words. (Have the colour cue close to your eyes to encourage eye contact while listening to the story.)

First, practise without the story by encouraging children to speak on cue. Keep it fun and make sure that less confident children become familiar with the words. Now read the whole story. Children will benefit from doing this more than once, or by swapping parts.

Special support
Use *peer support* and *alter the pace* to give the child time to respond.

Extension
Older children can play a spoken version of 'Consequences'. One child starts a story and a partner continues it, taking it in turns.

AGE RANGE
Five to seven.

GROUP SIZE
In pairs and small groups.

LEARNING OBJECTIVE FOR ALL THE CHILDREN
● To adopt appropriate roles in small groups.

INDIVIDUAL LEARNING TARGET
● To speak or communicate in a simple role play.

What a performance!

Developing imaginative language can be both challenging and fun for a child with cognition and learning needs.

What you need
A list of traditional-tale character pairs (for example, Hansel and Gretel; Red Riding Hood and the Wolf; Big Billy Goat Gruff and the Troll); a list of traditional story scenes; a spacious area; simple drama clothes and props.

Preparation
Display your list of character pairs. Prepare situations from familiar stories. Choose dramatic scenes or add new twists to the plots, all offering scope for four characters. These are examples:
● The Three Bears return to find their porridge has been eaten.
● Alice, now in Wonderland, comes across a strange group of people having tea.
● Cinderella and her two stepsisters try on the slipper for the prince.

What to do
Begin the session dressed for the theatre! Make an obvious change to your dress: a hat, cloak or bow tie. Explain that you're ready for a trip to storyland and you hope to see… (display your character pairs).

The children, with a partner, must choose a pair and decide which character they will each become. On your signal, they go into role, making up dialogue as they go along. Move around the area and pause to watch and listen to pairs. Keep time short (one to two minutes), and offer support where needed. Repeat this paired improvisation a few times, giving partners time to decide which characters to play next, and then give the new signal to begin.

Then snowball from pairs to fours. Present the children with your prepared story situations. Allow three to five minutes for groups to choose scenes and individual characters from these story situations. They must decide what will happen, but not their words, as these should be improvised.

At a signal, groups should begin their scenes, with you as a wandering audience again. Finally, let the children perform for a larger audience: other groups or the whole class.

Special support
Adjust the response in order to keep it simple and *keep it concrete*, depending on the child's level of understanding. This is a lovely activity for *extending imagination* especially if you take time to prepare the child with cognition and learning difficulties first, thereby *engaging attention* and setting *clear expectations*.

Extension
Older children can write or improvise their own plays and can attempt to 'direct' other children.

AGE RANGE
Seven to nine.

GROUP SIZE
Whole group and small groups.

LEARNING OBJECTIVE FOR ALL THE CHILDREN
● To make contributions, speaking audibly and listening actively.

INDIVIDUAL LEARNING TARGET
● To take a turn in a speaking and listening activity during circle time.

A magic wand

Circle time **provides an excellent way for children to develop attention and confidence.**

What you need
Six or seven small home-made wands; a display of useful headings linked to money-raising ideas, such as *raffle, concert, odd jobs, selling.*

Preparation
Display your list. Keep it limited, so that the children have scope for their own ideas.

What to do
Sitting in a circle, introduce the discussion topic, for example: the school Red Nose Day is coming and your class needs money-raising ideas. Build-up speaking confidence in children by keeping early contributions brief. Use a magic wand to empower people to talk: whoever holds the wand speaks, everyone else listens. You should start off by saying, 'We could make cakes.' Then pass on the wand.

When the wand returns to you, focus on one suggestion – perhaps a raffle. Ask the children to make points for and against a raffle. Repeat the process for another suggestion – perhaps selling biscuits. Encourage longer contributions by allowing the children to hold the wand for longer. Stress eye contact and attentive listening. When you regain the wand, model active listening, asking a question about something one of the children has said.

Your discussion should have produced a few good proposals. Divide the class into smaller groups of six to eight children, and assign each group a proposal. Each group prepares the case for that proposal. These groups will benefit from the same organisation: sitting in a circle, using a magic wand and making eye contact. Group members will eventually make their comments to the larger circle, so they need to decide on the order in which they will speak.

After ten minutes, re-form the large circle, with group members sitting near one another. When it is that group's turn to speak, each child should have something to say. After the cases are made, let the children ask questions. You are the impartial judge. Which activity will you choose?

Special support
This activity sets *clear expectations* for speaking and listening and also uses the speaking wand to *keep it concrete.* Encourage a *personal best* from any child with cognition and learning needs and use *shaping* to extend the length and quality of the utterances.

Extension
Once you have chosen a project, invite the children to prepare a spoken presentation for parents, detailing how the class will raise money and what support is needed from home.

AGE RANGE
Seven to nine.

GROUP SIZE
Whole class, in pairs, small groups.

LEARNING OBJECTIVE FOR ALL THE CHILDREN
● To use language to structure information.

INDIVIDUAL LEARNING TARGET
● To use a simple mnemonic to remember the order of information.

Elephants always remember

Mnemonics **are a powerful way of aiding memory, especially when the children have made them up themselves.**

What you need
A prepared collection of spelling mnemonics; individual copies of photocopiable page 51; dictionaries (optional).

Preparation
Make up some simple spelling mnemonics. Choose an information subject for the children's group mnemonics.

What to do
Present the children with a mnemonic: for example, *Hippos always love floods*. Explain that a mnemonic uses the initial letters of its words to aid memory. Ask what this spelling mnemonic would help someone to remember. (The spelling of *half*.) A spelling mnemonic can be funny, unusual or linked to the word's meaning – but it must be memorable. Make up some other simple spelling mnemonics with the children. The children, in pairs, could now use photocopiable page 51 for the rest of this session. One of the following scenarios could be used for a future activity:
● You need to remember some information in the correct order. (Perhaps the colours of the rainbow or names of Tudor kings.)
● You want a Reception class to remember the correct order of the seasons, or months of the year or days of the week.

Provide the necessary information orally, with the children listening and noting key facts. Organise the children into small groups. Each group must make up a mnemonic for the order of the information. The children could link mnemonics to themes, such as animals or food; or use a dictionary for inspiration, when an initial letter proves tricky. Move among groups, helping and encouraging the children to enjoy using language imaginatively.

Encourage oral work, one speaker trying out the mnemonic on the rest of the group. Could a word be improved? Would a change make the mnemonic more memorable? Can another member of the group solve the problem? Move from group to group, making an audio recording. Then hold a class listening session. Which mnemonic would you use?

Special support
Take care with *grouping:* make sure that groups are small enough for children with difficulties to feel involved. *Improve memory skills* by combining the mnemonic with a picture to aid visual memory.

Extension
Link this to a class spelling project. Find out the twenty most often misspelled words, either when spelling aloud or writing. Ask the children to invent and display a mnemonic for each difficult word.

AGE RANGE
Nine to eleven.

GROUP SIZE
Whole group, small groups, pairs and individuals.

LEARNING OBJECTIVE FOR ALL THE CHILDREN
● To use a range of oral techniques to present a persuasive argument.

INDIVIDUAL LEARNING TARGET
● To read from a prepared report.

Words can count

Some children with cognition and learning needs are better at reading than speaking. You can use this to help their understanding.

What you need
Proposals for the school council (see below); persuasive language (such as, *obviously, you must, surely, inevitably*); logical connectives (for example, *therefore, consequently, as a result, in order that*); a written paragraph, arguing your case for a job; paper and pens.

Preparation
Display examples of persuasive and logical language.

What to do
Pretend that you are ringing up about a new job. You have two minutes to explain why you want the job and why appointing you would be a good idea. Make your end of the conversation twice:
● badly – umming and aahing as you speak
● well – clearly, persuasively and logically, because you are reading a prepared paragraph.
Talk about the improvements when using a pre-prepared text.

Set the children this scenario. The school council is considering making a change to the school. It will listen to one proposal at its next meeting. What would be a good idea? Display possible proposals: a class water fountain; less homework; new school uniform; different school sports; better furniture; a separate playground for Years 5 and 6; a larger cloakroom.

The school council will be swayed by delivery. Remind the children of examples of logical connectives and persuasive vocabulary. Put the children into groups of about six. Suggest that group members choose a range of proposals. Each group member will support one proposal, but will only have about two minutes to speak to the rest of the group. Words must be effective and persuasive, so writing words in advance, checking, revising and practising should bring the best results.

Allow writing time, offering support and ideas where needed. When the writing has been completed, let the children use talk partners for advice and practice. Finally, ask the children to read their speech to their group. Is there one speech that wins the group vote?

Special support
Support the child through *small-group tuition* to write a simple passage and check understanding at this point. Then encourage the child to read this back to the group.

Extension
Extend this activity into a simple debating activity, allowing the children time to plan therir arguments in advance.

AGE RANGE
Nine to eleven.

GROUP SIZE
Whole group, small groups, pairs.

LEARNING OBJECTIVE FOR ALL THE CHILDREN
● To use and explore different question types.
● To practise and extend vocabulary.

INDIVIDUAL LEARNING TARGET
● To use descriptive language with a partner.

Any questions... any answers?

Abstract vocabulary sometimes has to be taught to a child with cognition and learning needs. Here is an activity that allows you to do this.

What you need
Copies of photocopiable page 52; six to 12 bags; a variety of objects (for example: a vegetable, a fruit, a piece of bread, a leaf, a fir cone).

Preparation
Place the objects in the bags. Stick copies of page 52 on to card (enough so that each child will have one), and cut out the pictures.

What to do
With your back to the class, describe one of the objects in your bag, without giving its name or too much information. Limit yourself to about five descriptive statements, for example, for an apple, you might say: *It fits inside my hand. It feels smooth. It looks polished. It is green. It is found outdoors and indoors.*

Let the children ask ten questions. Can they guess the object's identity? Repeat the game a few times. Discuss how the children found the answers. Thought-storm useful features of your descriptions, for example: texture, colour, size and smell. Identify which questions were most helpful. Point out the value of varying question types.

Put the children into groups of about six. Choose one person in each group to sit with their back to the others. Give that child a bag containing a mystery object. Each member of the group can ask the object holder one question. Can the group identify the object?

Repeat the game, using the picture cards made from the photocopiable sheet. Ask the children, in pairs, to sit back to back. Each partner must focus on a picture card. In five or six statements a child describes the object to the partner. Can the partner guess it? Eavesdrop on some of the descriptions, offering help to children with difficulties. If partners cannot guess from the descriptions, they can ask five or six questions. Do the answers give away the identity?

Come together as a whole class, and let some children make descriptions using the picture cards or by looking at objects around the class. Allow fewer questions. Have skills improved?

Special support
Keep it concrete by familiarising any child with difficulties with the actual objects first. Reduce *choices* by starting with a choice of only two or three objects to identify.

Extension
Develop the activity in pairs with one child describing an object and the other drawing what is being described on to a pad of paper. How good was the description?

Magic mishap

Section A

Here is the complete story to read aloud. Phrases in bold indicate where the children should say the words.

It was a new school year at the School of Wizardry. Already Samir's cat had caught measles, his best friend had turned purple and there had been **a terrible disaster**. Samir had made **the wrong spell**! During one of the magic lessons, Samir pointed **a magic wand**. Learner wizards were not allowed to aim **a magic wand** at anyone. Can you guess who Samir's wand was pointing at? **It was their teacher!** Then Samir said the words: '**Under the sea! Under the sea!**' Of course what he should have said was: '**Open Sesame! Open Sesame!**'

Because of his mistake, **a terrible disaster** happened: Samir made a shrinking, fishy spell. Can you guess who shrank and became fishy? **It was their teacher!** Now their teacher was stuck inside a goldfish bowl! The learner wizards tried spells.

'**Abracadabra! Abracadabra!**' shouted Sidney.

'**Open Sesame! Open Sesame!**' screamed Millicent.

It was no good. Samir and Millicent mixed up a magic potion. They put EVERYTHING in it and waved **a magic wand**. The learner wizards said all the magic words they knew. '**Abracadabra! Abracadabra!**' made the water in the fishbowl go blue. '**Open Sesame! Open Sesame**!' added yellow to the water.

Then they heard a watery voice. **It was their teacher!**

'You're making me feel sick,' complained the teacher fish. 'I am in here because somebody made **the wrong spell**, and pointed **a magic wand** at me and said, "**Under the sea! Under the sea!**" Now you have turned me green! This is **a terrible disaster**! Get me out of here!'

Can you rescue the green teacher fish?

Section B

Here are the children's speaking parts. Copy and display these words. Colour the squares to match your colour-coding.

☐ a terrible disaster   ☐ Under the sea! Under the sea!

☐ the wrong spell   ☐ Open Sesame! Open Sesame!

☐ a magic wand   ☐ Abracadabra! Abracadabra!

☐ It was their teacher!

Cognition

Spelling mnemonics

Read these mnemonics. Then make up new ones. Try them on a partner.

Tear
Tom's elbows are ripped

T<u>iny</u>_____ <u>el</u>ephant_____ a_____ r_____

T_____ e_____ a_____ r_____

Keys
Keep every Yale safe

K_____ e_____ y_____ s_____

Fruit
Fleas race up inside trousers

F_____ r_____ u_____ i_____ t_____

Heard
His ears are rather droopy

H_____ e_____ a_____ r_____ d_____

Gnash
Giraffes need awfully small hats

G_____ n_____ a_____ s_____ h_____

Honest
Harry otter never eats silly tadpoles

H_____ o_____ n_____ e_____ s_____

t_____

Guess what I am?

orange	daffodil	fire engine	traffic lights
banana	daisy	ambulance	tinfoil
sun	lemon	cloud	postbox
zip	ladybird	newspaper	comb
computer	carrot	Christmas tree	squirrel

Cognition

READING

When teaching reading to children who have cognition and learning needs, spend time *checking level* and *assessing learning style* when you first get to know them so that you can set out with *clear expectations* and minimise any feeling of failure. For example, children who have Down's syndrome may be strong visual learners and can make good progress using word sight, though their understanding of what they have read will need more support. In fact, there are approaches for teaching reading to improve language that build on these children's strengths in order to support areas of weakness (contact www.downsed.org for more information). Most children with learning needs benefit from an approach using SMC teaching for reading and you should find another book in this series helpful: *Activities for Including Children with Dyslexia and Language Difficulties* by Hannah Mortimer and Eileen Jones (Scholastic). The golden rule for children with these kinds of needs is to check constantly for understanding – some children who read with technical fluency may be 'hyperlexic', meaning that their ability to read exceeds their ability to comprehend written text.

Check that the texts you use have appropriate content and level for the child with cognition and learning needs, *breaking steps down* and *using the right language* for their level of ability. *Mind mapping* can be an excellent way to summarise written information and can assist a child's memory and recall. Where you have a comparatively strong reader, written texts can be used to improve memory skills. For example, you can teach a child to read lists and written aides-mémoires in order to help them remember procedures or to improve personal organisation.

Usually, children with cognition and learning needs benefit from the same approaches for learning to read as any other child so long as you make sure that the approach is *structured*, *multi-sensory* and

cumulative. However, for older children, make sure that the content is age-appropriate even if the level is simple, so that they remain motivated. Providing reading material that links to a hobby or personal interest can sometimes improve self-motivation. Look for opportunities for developing paired or shared reading, using *peer support* or a parent or carer. In paired reading, the child chooses the text, reads it out loud and prompts the partner when a new word is needed. In shared reading, both read out loud together at a steady rate and the child then hears the correct version of any word that they have not been able to read independently.

AGE RANGE
Five to seven.

GROUP SIZE
Small group.

LEARNING OBJECTIVE FOR ALL THE CHILDREN
● To read on sight high frequency words specific to graded books matched to the abilities of reading groups.

INDIVIDUAL LEARNING TARGET
● To identify key words from a reader.

Pond fishing

Visual learners will enjoy this fishing game involving word sight and key words.

What you need
Individual magnetic fishing rods (a stick with a piece of string with a magnet attached); about 20 to 25 fish-shaped word cards, each with a paper clip attached; two large plastic hoops.

Preparation
Write a high frequency word from current reading material on one side of each fish.

What to do
Work with a small group of about six children of similar reading ability, perhaps a group currently using the same reading book. Tell them that they are going fishing today! Explain that the fish are swimming face down in the water, so it is difficulty to identify them. The children can catch them with magnetism but, to keep them, they must identify them. If a fish is identified, it stays caught!

Scatter the word cards face down in the ponds (the large hoops). Let the children, using their fishing rods, take turns at fishing. When they catch a fish, they must turn it over and read the word. If they can read the word they catch, they keep it; otherwise the fish is thrown back into the hoop. Let the children make a pile of caught fish beside them. Who is the star fisherman of the day?

Collect all the fish and play a circle game. Deal the fish word cards among the children. Explain that the aim of this game is to lose fish, not to gain them. The winner will be the person with none left. The children are only allowed to return a fish when you call for it. Do this by playing a form of 'Bingo', but call for words not numbers. Think of novel ways to do your 'Bingo' calling, for example, by giving a meaning clue or providing the starting sound.

When a child has an appropriate word, they must hold it up and read it. Only if they are correct can they throw the fish into the pond. Play a final game of pond fishing. Have the children become better fishermen?

Special support
This activity can form part of your *structured, multi-sensory and cumulative* literacy teaching for a child with cognition and learning needs. Simply make sure that the child's words build on the right *starting points* for that child, *checking level* and *breaking steps down* as you need to.

Extension
You can extend this game by using more advanced, irregular or polysyllabic words. Children can also make up their own fish cards of words they wish to learn.

AGE RANGE
Five to seven.

GROUP SIZE
Small group, whole group.

LEARNING OBJECTIVE FOR ALL THE CHILDREN
● To secure identification, spelling and reading of initial sounds in simple words.

INDIVIDUAL LEARNING TARGET
● To hear the initial letter sound within a word.

Sound searchers

Children with learning needs may lack confidence and require motivating. Here is an activity that makes learning early phonics fun!

What you need
Pictures of familiar objects; cards coloured on one side.

Preparation
Make sure that you have sets of blank colour cards whose colours begin with the same sound, for example: green/gold/grey; pink/purple; blue/black/brown; red/rainbow (a picture of a rainbow).

What to do
Working with a small group will allow more progress with individual children and greater participation in each game. Sit in a circle and begin by asking the children to add to your alliterative rhymes. For example: *Hungry Harry has a... (hamburger). Silly Sarah swaps some... (socks).*

Have the children noticed something special about the rhymes' words? (Most of them begin with the same sound.) Ask the children to take a name (for example, *Jemima*). Make sure that there is variety among initial letter sounds. Ask the children to add a description with the same initial letter sound (*Jolly Jemima*). Let the children do this with a partner, before sharing with the whole circle. Repeat the activity for words you have been trying to learn: days of the week, colours, months of the year.

Now give everyone a colour card, asking them to keep the colour a secret. Check that each child can identify their colour. Explain that you are going to play 'Take my place'. When it is a child's turn, they must say their colour. Is there someone whose colour has the same initial letter sound? They should then swap places.

Repeat the game so that children work with a different sound. Extend the game, using the object pictures. Change the format by calling out an initial sound: children whose objects start with it then have to identify themselves and swap places. Finally, scatter all the cards face down on the carpet. Ask the children to search for a matching pair. If they turn over a card and reject it, they return it to where it was. Everyone can hunt at once, or the children (or partners) can take turns. How long do the sound searchers take?

Special support
Use a key worker to *engage attention* and help a child with difficulties hear the first sound and then remember it. *Break steps down* so that the child also remembers what to do with the information they have remembered once you are playing the circle game.

Extension
You can design similar activities focusing on end sounds.

AGE RANGE
Seven to nine.

GROUP SIZE
Whole group, in pairs.

LEARNING OBJECTIVE FOR ALL THE CHILDREN
● To write in complete sentences.

INDIVIDUAL LEARNING TARGET
● To assemble individual word cards in order to build up a sentence.

Scrambled sentences

Kinaesthetic learners will benefit from sentence-construction games. Here is an idea to help.

What you need
Paper and envelopes; individual whiteboards; plenty of white paper or card for each child; pens; washing line and pegs; computer and interactive whiteboard (optional).

Preparation
In clear writing, write sentences of six to ten words, for example: *fat sausages do sizzle and burn in hot frying pans.* Photocopy and cut out the words in each sentence. Put the scrambled set of words for one sentence in an envelope (one set for two children).

What to do
Give each pair of children an envelope containing a set of words. Ask the children to construct a sentence of at least three words. Verify the sentence before the children record it in writing. Then they should try to make a new sentence. This allows children to work at different speeds, and for you to provide extra support.

Now peg up the words – in a scrambled order – on the washing line, and let the children re-order them to display their results. Sentences could include: *sausages do sizzle; sausages burn in hot fat; frying sausages sizzle in hot pans*, and so on.

Use the sentences to reinforce sentence-level work: punctuation at the end of a sentence, verb function and adjectives. Repeat the exercise with scrambled versions of other sentences, for instance: *sensible and sweet cats drink fresh white milk* and *loud, popular parrots shout and squawk in all noisy shops.*

For collaborative work, use a computer and interactive whiteboard. Make trial and error fun, as children correct your deliberate mistakes by moving words with a finger or electronic pen. Ask the children, independently or with a partner, to write a sentence of six to ten words. Once the sentence has been checked, let them write it on plain paper or card. The children should cut out the words, jumble them and swap with another pair of children. How many different sentences can the other pair make? Finally, challenge the children to use all the words. Do the scrambled sentences return to normal?

Special support
Use a key worker to work in a small group with any children with difficulties at first, starting with a very simple three-word sentence. Gradually build up the length and complexity of the sentence, until these children are ready to join in with the large-group activity.

Extension
You can also plan activities based on scrambled stories in order to help children develop sequences of ideas.

AGE RANGE
Seven to nine.

GROUP SIZE
Whole group.

LEARNING OBJECTIVE FOR ALL THE CHILDREN
● To write instructions.

INDIVIDUAL LEARNING TARGET
● To refer to a written list in order to get organised for the school day.

Remind me again

Getting organised can be hard when you have memory difficulties. Reading aides-mémoires can help with this.

What you need
Individual copies of page 60; aides-mémoires linked to your day (examples supplied); computers (one between two) if available.

Preparation
Make enough copies of photocopiable page 60, one for each child.

What to do
Share your problems with the children! Explain that you have a lot of morning jobs. For example: switch on computers; write the date on the board; check which teacher is on duty, make spelling lists; check homework; write work on the board for children who have nothing to do; ring the bell and bring children in from the playground.

Explain that, because your memory is poor, you need memory prompts or aides-mémoires. These are short, quick to write, easy to recall, and have enough detail to tell you what you have to do. Written as instructions, each begins with an imperative verb, for example:

Write the date on the board. List the work so no one's bored.
Do the spellings in a list. Make sure homework is not missed.
Computers ready – one, two, three. Check for duty – is it me?
What's the time? Ten to nine. Ring the bell, keep in line.

Let the children use photocopiable page 60 to practise making up aides-mémoires. First they should complete the list of jobs and then make up an aide-mémoire for each. What other school jobs do the children have to remember? Consider situations or times of the day: pre-assembly; lunchtime; trips from school; getting out, assembling and putting away PE apparatus in the hall. Focus on one or two. Ask the children, with partners, to list six jobs. What aides-mémoires can they devise? Encourage oral and rough written drafts.

Alternatively, using a computer would allow one partner to suggest words while the other writes, and changes of mind would be easier to cope with. Emphasise the need to write in the form of instructions, using imperative verbs at the beginning. Finally, let the children share some of their finished work.

Special support
Keep it simple for a child with difficulties by focusing on the list of jobs. Rather than the written aide-mémoire, use pictures or digital-photograph sequences to serve as a visual aide-mémoire.

Extension
A display board with an aide-mémoire relevant to school life from every child would make a helpful and interesting classroom resource.

AGE RANGE
Nine to eleven.

GROUP SIZE
Whole group or small group.

LEARNING OBJECTIVE FOR ALL THE CHILDREN
● To evaluate a book by referring to details and examples in the text.
● To analyse the features of a good opening.

INDIVIDUAL LEARNING TARGET
● To select and read a book, reporting back on why it was enjoyable.

Rave reviews

Children with cognition and learning needs may need your support to develop reading for pleasure.

What you need
Textbook; ten to 20 different novels or short stories; photocopies of each first page; about four copies or photocopies of each story or opening chapter.

Preparation
Make sure that the books are of varying difficulty and genre, to cater for the whole class. Familiarise yourself with *shared reading* (see page 53 for details).

What to do
Explain that you want the children to be book reviewers. You want to discover what appeals to them and why. (You could use whole novels, but the task will be more manageable with opening chapters or short stories.)

Discuss the need to find books to suit our personal reading levels. Model how to identify this reading level: read a paragraph aloud from a technical book, stumbling over many of the words. Point out that you cannot cope with half of this book's words. Are you keen to carry on? (No!) Talk about 'frustration level': you must be able to read eight out of every ten words otherwise the book is too frustrating. Explain *shared reading*. Suggest it as a way to make an assessment.

Organise the children into groups of about six. Give each group a pile of photocopied opening pages. Allow browsing and reading time for the children to make an individual, partner or small-group choice. Stress that they are making a commitment to read the rest of the story or opening chapter.

With sufficient copies, everyone can read their chosen story or chapter at the same time; otherwise, groups can take turns over a number of lessons. Ask the children to make notes on their views, supporting them with textual references.

Finally, in whole-class or small-group book clubs, ask the children to report back to their peers about what they liked about their story or chapter. The children could then record their views in a class reading journal.

Special support
Use a key worker or *learning mentor* to monitor the reading level of a child who has difficulties to ensure that they are not reading in their frustration level. This might involve widening your resources so that all children have a good range of choice.

Extension
Organise a reviews file to go in your reading area. Encourage the children to select books to suit their interest and reading level.

AGE RANGE
Nine to eleven.

GROUP SIZE
Whole group.

LEARNING OBJECTIVE FOR ALL THE CHILDREN
● To write summaries of books or parts of books, deciding on priorities relevant to purpose.

INDIVIDUAL LEARNING TARGET
● To draw a simple cartoon to represent the main sequence of a written story.

Cartoon stories

Here is a motivating activity for helping children to précis and summarise what they have read.

What you need
Examples of cartoon stories, for instance, *Asterix* by René Goscinny and Albert Uderzo (Orion); individual copies of photocopiable page 61; A4 sheet (per child) for a storyboard of cartoon frames.

Preparation
Make enough copies of photocopiable page 61, one for each child.

What to do
Invite the children, in pairs, to read the extract from page 61. Ask them to discuss what is happening and to decide on six to ten main points. Let partners snowball into larger groups of four to share ideas. Move among the groups, helping and supporting as necessary.

Now investigate cartoon stories, showing the children some examples. Identify important features of this story form:
● an emphasis on pictures rather than words
● the use of separate frames or boxes
● the use of picture detail to move the story along
● a caption or short sentence used with each frame.

Set the following scenario: Jacqueline Wilson has agreed to the publication of an extract from her best-selling novel. However, the 'magazine editors' (the children) want to publish the extract in cartoon form. Point out that words and space will be limited, but main events from the extract must still be included. Unimportant events should be left out, and picture detail will have to do much of the storytelling. Pictures could include: the girl throwing money; getting out the scrapbook; removing sellotape from the scissors and cutting out pictures; playing at being a Victorian girl; drawing the house; Dad coming in; the girl rushing out of the bedroom; Dad, Mum and the girl in the living room.

The 'editors' will need to think carefully about the number of frames they use (about six to eight), content, and the wording for appropriate captions. Could some frames use speech bubbles? Could a time connective be added to the corner of a frame? Encourage the children to use their own words for the captions, not those contained in the extract. Ask the children to compare and share their final results. Make a display of the cartoons.

Special support
Break steps down by focusing on one or two frames only at first.

Extension
Use what you have learned together to print a class comic. This should be planned ahead, page by page and frame by frame, perhaps by an 'editorial committee' of children!

Aides-mémoires

Sports day is coming. Finish writing this list of jobs you must do to be prepared.

Get up early

Go to gym

Practise _____

Do _____

Improve _____

Learn to _____

Buy _____

Collect _____

Look for _____

Start _____

Stop _____

Now, in your books, write aides-mémoires to jog your memory about the jobs. These could help you get started

Get up early every day,

Go to gym _____

Practise running in a lane,

Ignore the cold _____

Do ten press-ups every night

Make sure _____

Stop eating chocolate every lunch

_____

Extract from *Lola Rose*

by Jacqueline Wilson

I threw the rest of the money at her and went off to my bedroom to work on my scrapbook. I started cutting up my new magazines, though Kenny had been at my scissors and they were all gummed up with sellotape. I picked all the mucky little sticky bits off the blades, my teeth clenched. Then I carefully cut out a Victorian doll with a purple crinoline. I snipped my way round every little twist and turn of her full frock and steered very slowly around her tiny button boots and cut in and out of her fiddly little fingers. I pretended I was a Victorian girl in a big purple dress and this was my matching doll. I had a little brother who was very obedient and adored his elder sister. We didn't have a papa.

    Then I cut out a tiny, toffee-brown cocker spaniel puppy with very floppy ears and a Siamese kitten with a delicate heart-shaped face and big blue eyes. These were our pets, Toffee and Bluebell. I cut some flowers from my birthday card box and a blue sky background and then I tried to draw a big Victorian house because I couldn't find a proper picture of one anywhere. I'm not very good at drawing so I just did a rough outline of a big house. I cut out girls' faces from *Girltalk* and stuck them looking out of all the windows, bordered by wax crayon purple velvet curtains. These were all my very best friends, Charlotte, Victoria, Emily, Evangeline and Jemima. It took me ages to think up special Victorian names.

    I was so lost in my scrapbook world that I didn't hear the front door bang. I didn't know my dad was home until I heard him call, 'Where's my princess then?'

    I shut my scrapbook up quick and shot into the living room. It's never a good idea to keep my dad waiting. But he'd called me princess, which was a promising sign. He might be in a good mood.

    He smiled as I rushed into the room. 'There's my girl!' he said, beckoning me over to his armchair. Kenny was already on his knee. Mum was snapping open a can of beer and pouring it for him.

    'Great, isn't it, Dad's home early,' she said.

    I breathed in. 'Hi, Daddy,' I said in this false small-girly voice.

    'Hi, Princess,' Dad said, and he patted the arm of his chair.

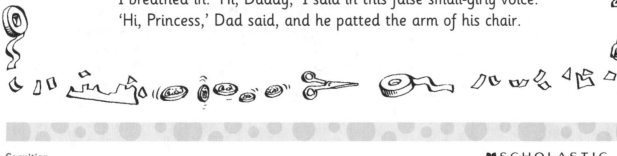

WRITING

Children who have global developmental delay may have genuine difficulties in holding a pen and pencil and controlling its movement. This strand of the National Curriculum has been included to provide you with some ideas for adapting activities, *adjusting the response* and providing *alternative means of recording* for a child with multiple difficulties. For children who cannot yet write, you can still include them by making use of a scribe (perhaps a partner or *adult support*), offering multiple choice, making *use of ICT*, and allowing verbal responses where appropriate. At the same time, you can carry out a *task analysis*, building up the early coordination skills that might eventually lead to simple pencil skills and early writing. Learning how to use a pincer grasp (in which the thumb and forefinger are isolated and used with precision), handling small objects, threading, stacking, building and keyboard games all lead on to the careful finger and hand movements needed for writing later on. Describing large circular movements in the air, during PE, with paint or when scribbling, all lead on to the early forms of mark-making used in writing. Start by assessing what the child can do now and then *break steps down* introducing new fine-motor skills step by small step. Sometimes there will be an occupational therapist who knows the child and who can support you with ideas or provide fine-motor therapy.

Some children with cognition and learning needs have learned how to write but are not well motivated, perhaps because they cannot see the point of it or because it is hard for them to produce a neat 'product'. These are the children who benefit from personally meaningful and motivating activities that expect their *personal best*, use *shaping* to improve legibility and *support planning and persistence*. Use additional *motivators* if necessary to 'kick-start' progress – a personal sticker system perhaps or the chance to display word-processed work for everyone to admire. The *use of ICT* is an excellent way of enabling weak writers to provide legible, organised and attractive written work to share with others.

Use triangular pencil grips to encourage the correct tripod pencil hold – you can mould one easily from sticky-tack or modelling material. Make sure you have paper and posture correctly set up for

children who are left-handed – there is an address on pages 95 to 96 for information and resources for left-handers. Finally, before a writing activity, try some simple 'brain gym' activities to get you all going – you will find information on pages 95 to 96.

SPECIAL NEEDS **in the primary years:** Cognitive and learning difficulties

AGE RANGE
Five to seven.

GROUP SIZE
Whole group.

LEARNING OBJECTIVE FOR ALL THE CHILDREN
● To form lower-case letters correctly in a script.

INDIVIDUAL LEARNING TARGET
● To trace an anticlockwise circle in the sand.

Which way?

Learning how to make and feel fine-motor movements can be a helpful way of learning writing movements.

What you need
Hall or large space; table; dark paper; sand or white powder (for example, icing sugar, flour, talcum powder).

Preparation
Cover a table with black paper dusted with sand or white powder.

What to do
Use a clock face to demonstrate 'clockwise' and 'anticlockwise'. Explain to the children that they are going to use anticlockwise movements. Introduce the children to the following activities.

● **Follow-my-leader**
Lead the children in an anticlockwise tour of the room.
● **Moving cogs**
Split the class into groups in sections of the room. Appoint leaders, and ask them to lead their group in a smaller anticlockwise circuit, all starting at a different time. Let groups take turns to watch the other 'cogs'. Are they all moving in the right direction? Reduce the size of the groups to three, so that the children all gain experience of leading. Pretend that the class is one giant machine. Control the machine with *Stop* and *Start* instructions.
● **Follow-my-thumb**
Let the children work individually. Keep using *Stop* and *Start* instructions as the children hold their thumbs in front of them to guide them on individual anticlockwise walking tours. Using the left thumb could be particularly helpful.
● **Letter formation**
Introduce letter formation. Stress the importance of starting points and explain that many lower-case letters start with anticlockwise movements (for example, *a, c, d, g*). In the air, form the letter *o*. Ask the children to copy. Extend the work to other letters. Ask the children to identify letters drawn in the air. Keep to lower-case letters requiring anticlockwise movement at the start.
● **Sand table**
Finish with a visible (but temporary!) display, as every child draws a letter in powder or sand. Does everyone start in the right direction?

Special support
Keep it concrete: put a finger puppet on to the left thumb. Show the child how to turn towards their thumb in order to start the anticlockwise motion.

Extension
Play a partner game, tracing letter shapes on to each other's back.

AGE RANGE
Five to seven.

GROUP SIZE
Whole group.

LEARNING OBJECTIVE FOR ALL THE CHILDREN
● To use simple poetry structures and to substitute own ideas and write new lines.

INDIVIDUAL LEARNING TARGET
● To print their name in different fonts or colours on the computer.

Words in print

The *use of ICT* allows even young children to produce writing they can feel proud of.

What you need
Computers (individual or one between two); poetry anthologies; selection of poems linked to familiar environments, such as home, school, the park. Suitable poems include 'Dinner Lady' by David Harmer, 'Playground Song' by Paul Cookson and 'Spring Cleaning' by Sue Cowling.

Preparation
Prepare a simple poem linked to a familiar setting. Leave lines incomplete for the children's ideas. This poem (line endings are supplied) would be a good example:

'School'
S is for _____(somersaults on the mat,)
C is for _____(colours in the paint pots,)
H is for _____(hexagon, one of the shapes,)
O is for _____(octopus on the spelling wall,)
O is for _____(orchestra in the hall,)
L is for _____(leaf on the teacher's plant.)
These are the alphabet blocks of my school.

What to do
Read poems linked to familiar environments. Display your example, leaving the lines unfinished. Share ideas for line endings. Let children use their ideas to complete it. Stress that there are no correct answers. Help them move from rough drafts to correctly spelled poems.

Explain that you want to publish an anthology of their poems. Show them poetry books. What do they notice about the poems' presentation? (Poet's name, legible font and so on.) Say you want this book to be as professional as possible, so it needs to be typed.

Revise ICT skills with the children. Introduce them to a range of fonts, colours and sizes. Teach them how to highlight text and then change the font, colour or size. Ask them to type their poems, keeping to the class's usual choice of font. Once the files are saved, let children experiment with different ways of presenting their text.

Encourage the children to help each other, whether or not they are sharing a computer. Children who lack confidence with computers will be glad of this support. Ask the children to look critically at their poem. Does the font selection or size need changing? Finally, remember the poet's name (their own!).

Special support
Take one familiar word, such as the child's name, and teach the child to experiment with different sizes, colours and types.

Extension
Select font sizes or types to go with the topic, such as a spiky font for a mystery poem or a colourful rounded script for a holiday poem.

WRITING · WRITING · WRITING · WRITING ·

AGE RANGE
Seven to nine.

GROUP SIZE
Whole group, in pairs.

LEARNING OBJECTIVE FOR ALL THE CHILDREN
● To write alternative endings or sequels to traditional stories.

INDIVIDUAL LEARNING TARGET
● To write a simple sentence independently.

What happens to your Cinderella?

Children with cognition and learning needs require you to break written tasks down for them.

What you need
A short version of a traditional story or use the version of 'Cinderella' supplied below; pens and paper or computers (one between two).

Preparation
Prepare the story you have chosen to tell the children. Decide whether the children will use computers or pens and paper.

What to do
Read aloud a short version of a traditional story, or use this text:

> *Once upon a time, beautiful Cinderella had two ugly sisters. Cinderella was good and kind, but her sisters were rude and lazy. Cinderella's cruel stepmother made poor Cinderella work and work.*
>
> *Lovely Cinderella had one wish: she wanted to join everyone else at the palace ball. Suddenly, there was a knock at the door. When Cinderella opened it, she saw a kind-faced, tiny woman.*
>
> *'I am your fairy godmother, and I will grant you your wish,' she said. The tiny woman waved her wand. With a flash of light, beautiful clothes, a fine carriage and proud horses appeared. So happy Cinderella went to the ball.*
>
> *'Remember,' warned her fairy godmother, 'return by midnight.'*
>
> *When the clock struck twelve, flustered Cinderella ran from the ball and the handsome young prince. However, she dropped her slipper. The prince searched and searched until he found Cinderella. Then they lived happily ever after.*

Point out the traditional features of the story: the opening and ending; good and bad characters; use of adjectives; magic. Ask the children how the story could finish differently. (At midnight, Cinderella becomes ugly. The prince fails to find the slipper's owner.)

Ask the children to write an alternative ending or sequel, working in pairs. They can begin orally, suggesting ideas by contributing parts of sentences. Progress to written work, moving from sentence beginnings or ends to whole ones. At the end, they need to check what they have written. Are the sentences in the best order?

Special support
Use a *key worker* to help any child with significant difficulties to think of one clear sentence. Write it on to a strip and cut it into word sections. Help the child reassemble and copy out the sentence.

Extension
A class story-reading session using the final versions would be fun.

AGE RANGE
Seven to nine.

GROUP SIZE
Whole group, in pairs.

LEARNING OBJECTIVE FOR ALL THE CHILDREN
● To understand how writers create imaginary worlds.

INDIVIDUAL LEARNING TARGET
● To plan a short independent piece of writing using a mind map.

Fantasyland

Mind mapping **is a powerful way to help planning when writing. This activity teaches children this approach.**

What you need
Individual copies of photocopiable page 69; paper and coloured pens for the children's mind maps; individual whiteboards or rough paper; OHP.

Preparation
Display Section A of photocopiable page 69 on the OHP.

What to do
Explain that you are writing a story. Show the children your plan (Section A of photocopiable page 69) on the OHP. Explain that this is a mind map and that this is a useful way to stimulate story ideas, words and detail. Allow five minutes for paired discussion about the mind map. Share ideas as a class. Ask questions such as, 'What is the story's main subject?'; 'What are the main sections?'; 'What detail is planned?'; 'Where should the story start?'

Explain how mind maps work: an important word is written on a long line or branch; shorter branches show connections to the word on the main branch (this connection could be emphasised by using the same colour); letter size indicates a word's relative importance (words on the shorter branches are minor, extra thoughts about the larger word on the main branch). Ask the children if they think pictures are useful. Do they inspire ideas for the smaller branches?

Invite the children to discuss in pairs what they would write in one part of the story. Let them trial sentences for each other, orally or by writing on whiteboards. Encourage them to build on each other's ideas. Listen to their sentences and offer support where necessary.

Now set a theme for the children's story: an imaginary world. They will do their planning on a mind map. The children should either finish the map already started (Section B of photocopiable page 69) or make a new one. Encourage initial rough versions, before finalising words on a proper map. (This will help weak spellers.) Let partners 'read' their maps to each other – using complete sentences. Now the children should write a paragraph of their story, perhaps the beginning or a section they are excited by.

Special support
Children with reading difficulties will gain fluency when they have recorded ideas using *mind mapping*. They are also an excellent way of *improving memory skills* when revising. Keep the mind map simple for a child with cognition and learning needs.

Extension
Organise group reading and listening sessions so that the children can enter one another's imaginary worlds.

AGE RANGE
Nine to eleven.

GROUP SIZE
Whole group.

LEARNING OBJECTIVE FOR ALL THE CHILDREN
● To use the structures of poems read to write extensions based on these.

INDIVIDUAL LEARNING TARGET
● To make careful pen movements in a simple illumination.

Model manuscripts

Careful finger movements can be more fun when there is an interesting reason behind them.

What you need
Photocopiable page 70 (individual copies or one copy for OHP display); an example of letter illumination (such as an illustration from a history book of the Lindisfarne Gospels); paper and different coloured pens.

Preparation
Make one copy of photocopiable page 70 for OHP display or enough copies for all the children. Prepare a display area.

What to do
Ask the children to help you create an important school display: – creative writing to be judged by appearance as well as content. Point out that many people become careless with handwriting and the children's manuscripts must highlight the correct way to write.

Revise letter formation by drawing letters in the air. Ask the children to identify them. Continue in groups of three, one child taking over your role as teacher, while the other two identify the letter being drawn. Observe everyone's letter formation and help with individual problems.

Read the extract from 'The Song of Hiawatha' to the children. Then ask them to write their own poem based on what Hiawatha would hear, see or touch in your modern-day school. Share ideas, using Section B of the photocopiable sheet as a starting point. Will the children's writing retain the character of Hiawatha? Will they substitute a modern name? Will they put themselves into their poems? Ask them to draft ideas, phrases and lines. They could try out lines on a listening partner. Help correct spelling on final versions.

Most poets begin each line with a capital letter. Ask the children to follow this pattern as they copy out their poems for the display. A coloured pen would make each letter stand out. For the very first letter, suggest a beautiful illumination. Show the children an example of medieval illumination and point out how the illustration usually supports the text.

Special support
Supply a bold black pen to form the letter shape and then encourage careful pen strokes to complete the illumination around it. Use *shaping* techniques and encourage *personal best* in order to help the child with difficulties to obtain better pen control.

Extension
This display could become a permanent model for school handwriting. Children might like to take each letter in turn and make an alphabet frieze of illuminated letters.

AGE RANGE
Nine to eleven.

GROUP SIZE
Whole group, in pairs.

LEARNING OBJECTIVE FOR ALL THE CHILDREN
● To revise the language conventions and grammatical features of instructional texts.

INDIVIDUAL LEARNING TARGET
● To write a simple sequence of instructions with support.

Buried treasure

Writing that leads to something useful will carry more personal meaning for a child with learning needs.

What you need

An example instructional text for OHP display; sample instructions leading to places in classroom; yellow discs of card representing gold coins (two for each child); pens or pencils and paper.

Preparation

Display an instructional text on OHP. Use your classroom instructions or these computer instructions:
First make sure that everything is plugged in.
Then switch on at the wall.
Afterwards press the large, circular button at the top of the keyboard.
Check that a green light appears.
Wait until the screen displays the menu.
Use the mouse to operate the cursor.

What to do

Identify the essential features of an instructional text: present tense verbs; time connectives; imperative verb forms; imperatives close to sentence beginnings; a layout of separate lines.

Set a scenario: shipwrecked pirates have buried some of their treasure. These pieces of gold are in matching pairs; each pair has a its own symbol or pattern. The pieces of gold are worthless without the matching pair. The children will be given only one coin and written instructions leading to the matching one. Will they find it?

Share ideas on straightforward examples of written instructions, or perhaps incorporate rhymes or riddles. Now give each child two gold coins. First they must put their initials and an identifying matching sign, symbol or pattern on both coins. After hiding one coin, they write instructions for someone else to find it. Ask the children to exchange coins and instructions with a partner. Each child must now follow the instructions to find the matching coin.

If it is difficult to have everyone searching at once, let just one partner search. Set a time limit before partners swap over. If a search remains fruitless, instructions may need more detail, or individuals may need support. As children make their finds, ask them to write an explanation of how they did it.

Special support

Break steps down if you need to. Some children might find it helpful to draw a series of picture clues first and then write their sentences of instructions based on those.

Extension

Help the children agree a set of clear directions for a supply teacher joining their class or for a visitor to find their way to the classroom.

Mind maps

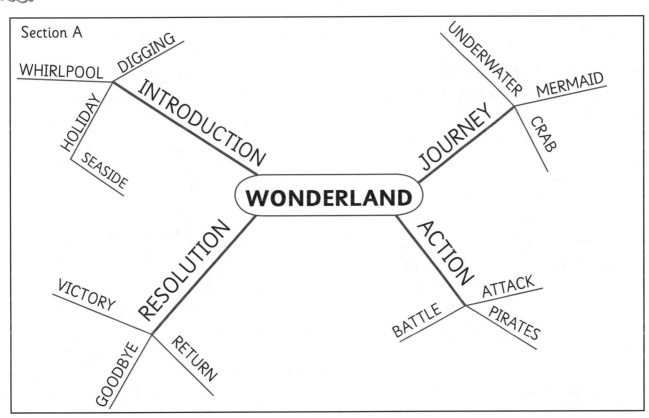

Section A

WHIRLPOOL · DIGGING

INTRODUCTION

HOLIDAY

SEASIDE

UNDERWATER · MERMAID

JOURNEY

CRAB

WONDERLAND

RESOLUTION

ACTION

VICTORY

GOODBYE · RETURN

ATTACK

BATTLE · PIRATES

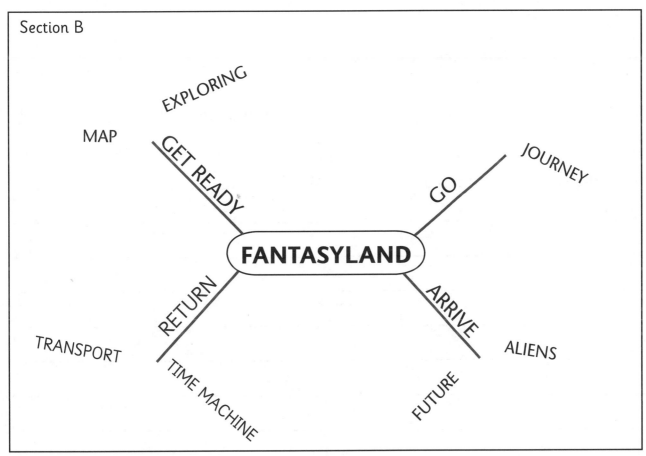

Section B

EXPLORING

MAP

GET READY

JOURNEY

GO

FANTASYLAND

RETURN

ARRIVE

TRANSPORT

ALIENS

TIME MACHINE

FUTURE

The idea and term 'mind map' is based on Tony Buzan's book *Mind Maps for Kids* (2003, HarperCollins)

Illuminated poetry

Section A

Hiawatha's childhood

At the door on summer evenings
Sat the little Hiawatha;
Heard the whispering of the pine-trees,
Heard the lapping of the water,
Sounds of music, words of wonder;
'Minne-wawa!' said the pine-trees,
'Mudway-aushka!' said the water.
    Saw the fire-fly, Wah-wah-taysee,
Flitting through the dusk of evening,
With the twinkle of its candle
Lighting up the brakes and bushes,
And he sang the song of children,
Sang the song Nokomis taught him.

*Extract from 'The Song of Hiawatha' by Henry
Wadsworth Longfellow*

Section B
Use these lines for ideas in your own verses.

In the classroom Monday morning

Sat the bright-eyed, waiting pupil;

Heard the tapping of the keypad,

Heard the _____

_____

_____

_____

_____

Saw the busy bee, the teacher,

Darting, buzzing 'round the classroom;

With the _____

_____

_____

_____

_____

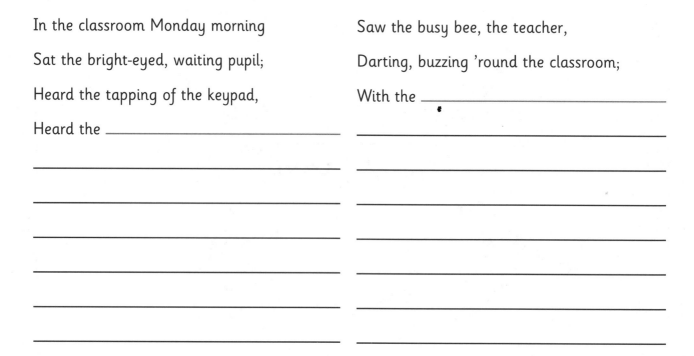

USING AND APPLYING MATHEMATICS

The attainment target for Mathematics 1, Using and applying mathematics, has been chosen both for the challenges and the opportunities that it presents for children with cognition and learning needs. In this section, there are activity ideas for helping children to use mathematics as an integral part of their school day and helping the child with cognition and learning needs to develop mathematical vocabulary, recognise pattern and quantity and begin to solve problems. The key is to *keep it concrete,* providing visual and sensory approaches for the children who cannot yet process number in the abstract sense. Again, it helps to *assess learning style* so that you can plan your teaching in a way that is *structured, multi-sensory and cumulative.*

Try to look for workbooks that allow a child to repeat and consolidate new mathematical concepts rather than to 'dot around' between different concepts. Learning new mathematical concepts can become repetitive and demoralising for a child unless you have a wide range of materials at your disposal or are prepared to design individual approaches. Remember to *check level* carefully: you will find yourself allowing the child to use counting aids, number lines and number squares much longer than you may be used to. Keep a number frieze in a prominent place so that a child with memory difficulties can use it to refer to, enabling them to recognise and copy numbers. Encourage certain children to stand up and move their finger along the line if using it as an aid to calculation – this movement helps to develop understanding. Some children appear to need sensory experiences of counting, handling, observing change in quantity, estimating and predicting long after they have passed the Foundation Stage – be prepared to borrow and develop practical resources to help these children develop a practical and concrete understanding of number.

Problem-solving for children with cognition and learning needs often requires a high level of *adult support* at first, though working within a small team or with a partner can be a useful way of including them in collecting the data. Try to find suitable roles within the team where each child can use and apply mathematics at their own level of ability and understanding. Encourage the asking of mathematical questions, either verbally or through experimentation ('I wonder what will happen if…?') as a first step towards being able to solve problems and answer them.

AGE RANGE
Five to seven.

GROUP SIZE
Whole group, small groups.

LEARNING OBJECTIVE FOR ALL THE CHILDREN
● To understand and use the vocabulary of comparing and ordering numbers.

INDIVIDUAL LEARNING TARGET
● To understand what is meant by more than and less than.

Mighty more and little less

Children with cognition and learning needs require you to link mathematical vocabulary with direct actions.

What you need
The hall or other spacious area; large PE hoops (two differently coloured hoops per small group); various items with at least ten of each (bats, balls, quoits); large *more* and *less* display signs; two PE bands – one red, one blue; individual whiteboards; individual *more than* and *less than* cards; individual copies of photocopiable page 78.

Preparation
Hang up the large signs *more* and *less*.

What to do
Place four balls under the *more* sign and place two under *less*. Keep demonstrating the difference in the two meanings using your other items. Involve the children, asking their advice about how many objects to put under whichever sign remains empty. Ensure that you sometimes begin at the *more* sign and sometimes at the *less* sign. Hang up two bands: red on one side of the room, blue on the other. Stand three children in the red team, seven in the blue. Let the class confer with partners to answer the following questions:
● Which team has more?　● Which team has less?
● How many more blues than reds are there?

Use different team members, numbers and questions. Give everyone an opportunity to answer. Allow thinking time, using individual whiteboards for the children to display answers (partners could still confer). Similarly, ask the children to hold up the appropriate card (*more than* or *less than*) for questions such as, 'Does the red team have more or less than the blues?'

Gradually extend the children's learning, by letting them take control of choosing the amounts. For example, assign six members to the blue team, but only two captains for the reds: the captains must pick a red team, making sure that there are more reds than blues.

Organise the children into small groups. Give each group two hoops of different colours and two labels (*more than* and *less than*). Provide a selection of items (bats, balls, quoits and so on). Ask each group to place a different number of an item inside the two hoops, with the appropriate label next to each. Develop the task by asking the group to prepare a statement using the words *more than* or *less than*. Reinforce the learning with the photocopiable worksheet.

Special support
Focus on just one concept first – *more*, using many different quantities.

Extension
Move on to working with the same concepts but using small tabletop apparatus.

AGE RANGE
Five to seven.

GROUP SIZE
Whole group, in pairs.

LEARNING OBJECTIVE FOR ALL THE CHILDREN
● To use mental addition and subtraction, simple multiplication and division to solve simple word problems involving numbers in 'real life'.

INDIVIDUAL LEARNING TARGET
● To use counting to solve practical problems.

Count the problems!

Here is an activity to help children with cognition and learning needs to generalise their mathematical learning to day-to-day events.

What you need
A selection of mathematical problems photocopied one for each pair of children.

Preparation
Prepare a list of problems reflecting your day in the classroom (see below for examples).

What to do
Talk about numeracy. Ask the children if they think numeracy is only for numeracy time. Can the children suggest other occasions in the day when numeracy is relevant? (Making teams, checking dinner money and so on.) Introduce the various mathematical problems that you prepared, for instance:
● There are 23 children in Mr Allen's class. If 13 of them are boys, how many are girls?
● The bus driver collects 8 children on the school bus, then 2 and then 12. How many children are there in total on the school bus? How many more children are needed to make the 23 in the class?
● Mr Allen must ask the children in his class to sit in pairs. How many pairs can he make from 23? Will anyone be left over?
● At lunchtime, the 23 children must share tables. If 10 children can sit at each table, how many full tables are there? How many children must sit at a table that is not full?
● If 12 children (out of 23) have a cooked lunch, how many bring sandwiches?
● At story time, there are only 16 chairs. If there are 23 children, how many have to sit on the floor?
● By home time, 22 chairs are scattered all over the classroom. The caretaker likes them kept in stacks of 3. How many stacks of 3 can Mr Allen make? How many chairs will be left over?

Judge how many problems to present at once: some children may benefit from having just one problem at a time. Let the children work with a partner, using discussion, mental operations and individual strategies before writing the answer. Can children explain how they solved a problem?

Special support
Keep it concrete by pointing out visual aids, such as number friezes and squares and times-tables charts. Use lower numbers in the problems.

Extension
Encourage children to 'translate' the problem into a mathematical equation. For example, problem one above would be 23 –13 = 10.

AGE RANGE
Seven to nine.

GROUP SIZE
Whole group.

LEARNING OBJECTIVE FOR ALL THE CHILDREN
● To check subtraction with addition.

INDIVIDUAL LEARNING TARGET
● To 'mark' and correct a simple piece of written mathematics.

That's a mistake!

Children need encouragement to organise and check their work – here is an idea to help.

What you need
Ten to 15 completed subtraction calculations – some of them with incorrect answers.

Preparation
Make an OHP display of your calculations for the end of the lesson, or list and photocopy them for every child.

What to do
Write three subtraction calculations on the board:
● 30 – 11 =   ● 39 – 12 =   ● 24 – 17 =

Allow the children two minutes to complete them; then write your three answers (deliberately making one of them incorrect). Compare the results. Hopefully, there will be disagreement. Ask how the children can check the answers. Suggestions may include counting aids such as fingers, bricks, number lines and squares. Ask if they can think of a mathematical operation that can be used. If they fail to suggest addition, leave the calculations and do some speedy mental work on addition and subtraction facts to 20. Make a point of repeating the same numbers (for example, say: 'What do you need to add to 6 to make 11?' and then say, '11 minus 6 equals?').

The children should eventually recognise that if two numbers in the completed subtraction calculation are added, then the starting number should be reached: the answer is added to the number subtracted. Check your original calculations with the children. When you reach your incorrect answer, show, by way of the check, that it is wrong. Point out the value of checking with an inverse operation.

Model other examples; then let the children complete some more subtraction calculations and check a partner's answers. Check the children's calculations and find out if they are sure of how to check the answers. (If children remain uncertain of the process, let partners work together, exchanging completed calculations with another pair for them to check.) Finish the lesson by displaying your completed subtraction calculations (with some deliberate errors) and say that you think some may be wrong. Ask the children to check your subtraction work by using addition. Can they find your mistakes?

Special support
Children with learning needs might find mental jumps hard; if they cannot work out the inversion rule for themselves, give them clear rules on how to check subtractions using addition, step by small step.

Extension
Once a child is confident with inversion, incorporate it into everyday maths work, challenging the child to spot mistakes and put them right.

AGE RANGE
Seven to nine.

GROUP SIZE
Whole group.

LEARNING OBJECTIVE FOR ALL THE CHILDREN
● To use all four operations to solve word problems in 'real life'.

INDIVIDUAL LEARNING TARGET
● To respond to a simple problem-solving task using multiple choice.

Eat your money's worth

The use of multiple choice can allow you to include children with learning needs in a problem-solving activity.

What you need
Menu with prices; individual whiteboards and pens.

Preparation
Create a café menu for display.

Menu			
All Day Breakfast	£1.95	Mixed salad	£1.22
Fish and chips	£1.95	Tea	22p
Cheese and tomato pizza	£1.65	Orange squash	30p
Sandwiches	£1.45	Cola	45p
Chips	74p	Apple pie	60p

What to do
Revise money, such as coin denominations, the conversion of pounds to pence, the number of pence in a pound, and how to use a decimal point. Make up simple word problems involving money. Say to the children, for example: 'You need to change your £5 note into pence. How many pence will you get?' Supply the answer, but in the form of multiple choice ('5000p or 500p?'). The children can use individual whiteboards to show you the correct answer (500p). Allow children to work with a partner if you think some of them will struggle, as this will help them to gain confidence.

Move progressively to harder problems, for example: 'Raj and his friends bought four football tickets for £84. How much was each ticket – £20, £21 or £22?' Ask how they worked out their answers and check if they are correct. Next, show the children the café menu. Explain that they have £5 to spend. Present three situations:
● They want an afternoon snack for four people.
● They want lunch for two.
● They will be in the café from 10am until 5pm. How will they feed themselves on £5?

Explain that there is no single correct answer to any problem: they just have to keep to budget! Let children work individually, unless partner support is essential. Afterwards, ask the children to compare answers with a partner. Can the partner spot any errors? Finally, ask the children to contribute – pictorially and with prices – to a class display of answers. Who has made the best use of £5?

Special support
Start by offering two *choices* that differ widely. This helps the child to make use of estimation and common sense.

Extension
Plan a budget for a class fund-raising event.

AGE RANGE
Nine to eleven.

GROUP SIZE
Whole group, in fours.

LEARNING OBJECTIVE FOR ALL THE CHILDREN
● To discuss the chance or likelihood of certain events.

INDIVIDUAL LEARNING TARGET
● To work as part of a team, gathering data.

Channel choice chance

Gathering data can include children at all levels of ability. In this activity, everyone has a 'job to do'.

What you need
Paper and pens; paper for graphs; bags containing six identical plastic coins (one bag per group of four children).

Preparation
Prepare a bag and six coins for each group of four children. Using six colours, put a dot on each coin. Place a coin of each colour in every bag.

What to do
Present the following scenario: your family argues about which TV channel to watch – BBC1, BBC 2, ITV, Channel 4, Channel 5 or Sky. So you have devised a system and assigned each channel a colour. You have put a blob of colour on six coins and placed them in a bag. Every evening someone in your family will pick one out, without looking. Whichever colour is picked will be the channel watched.

Introduce the term *hypothesis* (an unproved theory). Explain that you have given your favourite channel the colour green, as you have this hypothesis: *green will be picked out more frequently than any other colour.* Ask the children about the likelihood of this and to test your hypothesis with the following activity.

List the channels and assign colours. Organise the class into groups of four, providing each with paper, pens and a bag of six coins. Decide on a number of times for coins to be picked (for example, 50). The group must agree on the jobs to be shared: picking coins, identifying colours, and recording them on paper. Stress the need for a fair test. The groups should record their data in a quick and reliable way: for example, listing colours in the order they appear or using a tally system. Once groups have their data, demonstrate creating a bar line chart, labelling the vertical axis *frequency* and the horizontal axis *colours*. Ask the groups to do the same, every child or pair producing a graph.

Compare the class's outcome. Are the results similar? What do the children think would happen if they continued 50 more times? Let them try. Ask each group to explain what they have learned about frequency. (They should have discovered that your hypothesis was wrong, as chance always determined the colour picked.)

Special support
Encourage a child with cognition and learning needs to participate at whatever level is possible for them – such as recording with tally counts.

Extension
Move on to simple chance activities using dice – what is the chance of throwing two sixes?

AGE RANGE
Nine to eleven.

GROUP SIZE
Whole group.

LEARNING OBJECTIVE FOR ALL THE CHILDREN
● To identify and use appropriate operations to solve word problems involving numbers and quantities.

INDIVIDUAL LEARNING TARGET
● To contribute to complex problem-solving, step by small step.

Shopping spree

Children at this age can tackle quite difficult problems if you *break steps down* into smaller tasks.

What you need
A sheet of money problems (examples supplied); paper and pens.

Preparation
Make enough copies of the sheet of money problems, one for each child.

What to do
Set a scenario in which Year 6 has shopped for this year's school fete. The children have returned with the goods, shop bills, receipts and change. You, their teacher, need proper accounting done. The children have questions to answer!

Organise the class into small groups. Each group should discuss the problems; choose the most appropriate operations and methods of calculation; explain and record their solutions on paper, using numbers, signs and symbols; be prepared to explain orally how they solved the problem. Stress the benefit of tackling problems in small steps: for example, when finding the total of four numbers, only deal with two at once. Then ask your questions:

● *Super Store* has given four separate bills: £115.14, £2.71, £12.05 and £5.00. What is the total bill?

● *Worthwhile* sells everything in multi-packs. You need to know the cost of individual items: a bumper pack of crisps marked *10 for £3.80*; a bumper pack of lollipops marked *100 for £15.00*, and a multi-pack of chocolate cakes marked *5 for £2.55*.

● Some children went into *Cash Carry* with a £50 note. They bought 135 bottles of fizzy drink at 31p each. How much change should they have?

● The receipt from *Cut Price* lists the following: *£38.18 HALF PRICE; £131 HALF PRICE; £26.23 HALF PRICE; £283.20 HALF PRICE.* What were the full starting prices?

● *Quickbuy*'s bill is £90.00, but the shop gives schools 5% discount. How much discount will there be? What will the new bill be?

Set a time limit, accepting that groups will vary in the number of problems they tackle. Afterwards let groups present reports on their mathematical strategies and methods.

Special support
Check level and keep it simple: present one problem at a time and make sure it is at the right level for the child's ability. Make use of small groups and partner work to support a child with difficulties. *Keep it concrete* by using visual and tactile counting aids if necessary.

Extension
Certain children might like to try writing a simple set of accounts.

More than... less than

5 frogs

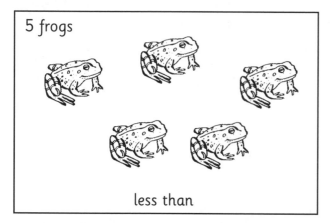

less than

6 ducks

more than

5 cats

_____ than

4 dogs

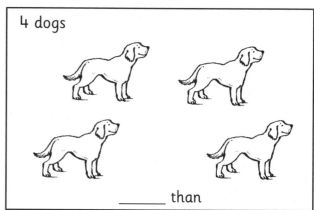

_____ than

___ houses

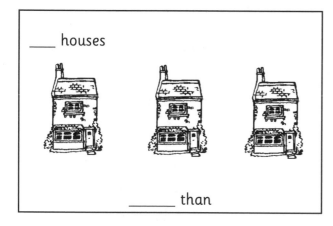

_____ than

___ doors

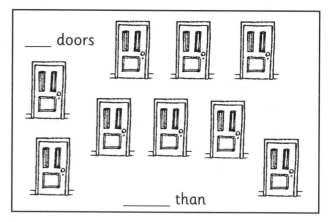

_____ than

Can you fill in the gaps? The first set has been done for you.

Finish this statement about one set of pictures:

There are more _____ than _____.

Cognition

SCIENTIFIC ENQUIRY

This strand of the curriculum has been included because of both the challenges and the opportunities it presents. Some children with cognition and learning needs tend to respond rather passively to their surroundings and 'wait for the world to come to them'. If you can plan scientific activities that help them to interact with materials and processes in an exploratory way, then you have a chance of helping them to become more active learners. At the early stages of scientific enquiry, they can be helped to link cause with effect, coming to see that the way they are interacting with materials directly influences what happens next. This can lead on to their learning how to make simple observations and to begin to 'ask questions', either through their words or through their actions. Presenting, considering and evaluating their evidence might be more challenging for them and you will need to find ways to *break steps down*, *keep it concrete*, *adjust the response* and find *alternative means of recording*.

At Key Stage 2, children typically learn to make links between ideas and to explain things using simple models and theories. They begin to plan ahead, deciding what evidence they need, how to obtain it and how to use it to test an idea. Some children with cognition and learning needs will find this degree of abstract thinking hard, yet can still be helped to pose simple questions: 'I wonder what will happen if ...' They can be helped to give feedback to others and to repeat actions to test whether the effects are the same. Set *clear expectations* during practical tasks and *use a key worker* if you need to ensure health and safety. *Support planning and persistence*, help the child to learn how to *sequence* actions and use *task analysis* to make practical investigation more simple. *Small-group tuition* might be a useful route, making use of *peer support*. Within a small team, children with cognition and learning needs can enjoy making useful contributions to data collection even if they need individual help when it comes to making sense of the data and

testing theories. This aspect of science – scientific enquiry – has been chosen because it actually teaches children how to learn and how to find out what they need to know about the world around them. Developed flexibly, it can be an invaluable part of the curriculum for the child with cognition and learning needs.

AGE RANGE
Five to seven.

GROUP SIZE
Whole group.

LEARNING OBJECTIVE FOR ALL THE CHILDREN
● To observe and describe different ways of moving.

INDIVIDUAL LEARNING TARGET
● To copy simple movements and use action words to describe them.

Get moving!

Here is a simple, practical activity that develops children's investigative skills at many levels of ability.

What you need
Large indoor space, such as the hall; music of your choice.

Preparation
Decide on the movement vocabulary to focus on.

What to do
Explain to the class that your PE dance session is going to investigate movement. Play music for the children to move to. Stop and start the music, as you give the children a series of clear, simple instructions (for example, *march; skip*). Let the children watch one another. Point out interesting movements, using relevant vocabulary. For example, 'Dwight is *twisting* his body'; 'Almyra is *swinging* her arms'; 'Carla is *pushing* one leg forward'.

Extend the range of actions and language (for example: *hop, jump, fast, slow, swerve, pull, spin, slide* and *turn*). Ask the children to work with a partner as you play a new piece of music. One partner will be the leader; the other must follow the movements. Then the children should reverse roles. Use some pairs as examples, commenting on and asking questions about their movements.

Repeat the activity with different music and the children facing each other. One partner is real; the other is only a mirror! Will the mirror work properly? Can the mirror reflect the partner's exact movements? Give the children a theme (such as: *Getting ready for school*). Allow rehearsal time before partners present their movement sequence to another pair.

Point out that PE lessons always start with a short warm-up. Can the children devise their own warm-up? Partners must work together, the speaker giving instructions for the listener to follow, and then reversing roles. Consider supplying a theme for the movements, such as *Playtime*. Encourage the children to talk to each other about their movements. Check that they have the appropriate vocabulary. Allow plenty of discussion and rehearsal time. Does the speaker use appropriate words? How does the listener move?

Special support
Children with cognition and learning needs should be able to respond to a simple mirroring activity, either as a model or a reflector. Use this as a time to emphasise action words, *using the right language* for the child's level.

Extension
Let the children present their movements to an audience – the whole class or a group. Explore simple ways of recording your movements, using paper or technology.

AGE RANGE
Five to seven.

GROUP SIZE
Whole group, small groups.

LEARNING OBJECTIVE FOR ALL THE CHILDREN
● To learn that some differences between ourselves and other children can be measured.

INDIVIDUAL LEARNING TARGET
● To cooperate within a small team in presenting simple evidence to others.

Spot the difference

Presenting evidence can be fun when it is linked to something the children really wish to show off.

What you need
Camera; wide-lined paper for graphs; different measuring apparatus (such as, weighing scales, rulers, measuring tape, measuring sticks).

Preparation
Take, develop and give out individual photographs of the children, but first gain consent from the children's parents or carers.

What to do
Ask the children to compare photographs with a partner. What differences can they spot? (Straight or curly hair; blue or brown eyes.) Share results. Introduce the word *variation*. Show the children written information about variation among teachers, for example: *Miss Brown take size six shoes; Mr Smith wears size eight. Mrs Shepherd and Mrs Khan both take size seven. Mr Patal wears size nine shoes, but Mr Evans needs an enormous size ten!*

Suggest presenting the information visually. Demonstrate making a block graph, with names on the horizontal axis, and shoe sizes on the vertical axis. Use a different colour for each teacher. Ask the children questions about the information on the graph, helping them with interpretation.

Now organise small teams (about four children per team). Explain that each team must measure a possible variation among themselves. Decide on the focus for the comparison. Possibilities could include: shoe or trainer size, hand span, hand length, shirt collar size, height or weight. Ask teams to plan work in advance, thinking about important issues such as: accuracy, how to measure, units of measurement, how to make comparisons fair (for example, measuring hand spans with or without hands stretched out) and so on.

Invite the children to make and write some predictions before they measure. (Do they guess that most of them will have the same shoe size?) Stress the need to work as a team, helping one another with measuring, checking, and keeping a written record. Written records then need to be converted into block graphs. Move among groups, supporting as necessary. Ask each team to return to its predictions. Were they correct? Can they now use their graphs to make four deductions? (For example, *Rio's hand span is bigger than Amy's.*) Ask teams to present information to one another – visually and orally.

Special support
Break steps down and set *clear expectations*: give any child with cognition and learning needs explicit instructions and help.

Extension
Explore ways of recording this kind of data using computer software.

AGE RANGE
Seven to nine.

GROUP SIZE
Whole group, small groups.

LEARNING OBJECTIVE FOR ALL THE CHILDREN
● To raise key questions about the diet of different pets.

INDIVIDUAL LEARNING TARGET
● To ask a simple question and find out an answer.

Pet questions

Asking questions is a central part of scientific enquiry – this small-group activity ensures there is a job for everyone.

What you need
Resource material about pets; computers (optional); pens and paper; paper large enough for posters; information on human dietary needs.

Preparation
Select or put together an example of clear information about our diet.

What to do
Show the children the information about our diet. Point out the clarity and ease of access of your information. How is the reader helped? (*Headings, questions, pictures and diagrams.*) Stress that lengthy, dense text has been avoided. Explain that you want to make posters with information of equal clarity about the diet of pets.

Organise small groups of children (four to six) and ask them to decide on a pet. Aim at variety, but you may need to limit choice to suit your reference material. Model a poster layout, with the pet's name in the centre of the poster and four or five lines springing from the centre leading to sections of information. Each section could have a question as its heading (for example, *How much liquid is needed?*). The information underneath would supply the answer. Each group must think about three aspects of the work: what questions to ask (the ones the reader will want answered); what the group already knows; and what they need to find out.

In order to decide about these work areas, group members need to discuss the topic. Remind them about important speaking and listening rules: taking turns to speak; listening attentively to one another; and building on one another's contributions. Suggest that the children use one another for different roles: they do not all need to make notes on every decision; they do not all need to work on each question. Will they research in pairs? Will someone be responsible for pictures? Stress the need to make notes that they will understand later, to use their own words, and to note page numbers from books or magazines if they plan to copy a picture.

Allow a further session for the children to do final versions of drawing and writing (perhaps making computers available) and sticking work on to their poster. Display the results and ask the children to think about how well questions were answered.

Special support
Keep groups small and make use of *adult support* or *learning mentors*. Make the work multi-sensory and *keep it concrete* by making use of pictures, writing and small-world models.

Extension
Write a class book on 'Finding the best pet for you'.

AGE RANGE
Seven to nine.

GROUP SIZE
Whole group, small groups.

LEARNING OBJECTIVE FOR ALL THE CHILDREN
● To make careful measurements of temperature at regular time intervals.

INDIVIDUAL LEARNING TARGET
● To read a thermometer.

Testing temperatures

Careful observation is a central part of data collection – here is a motivating activity to keep everyone focused.

What you need
Thermometers reading plus or minus degrees Celsius (one per two or three children); a list of noon-day temperatures in Celsius; squared paper for individual or group graphs; computers (optional); plastic beakers (one per group); two thermos flasks; different materials, for example: bubble wrap, foam rubber, layers of newspaper, socks, towelling, thick woollen knit and carpet.

Preparation
Place some thermometers around the classroom (a sunny window ledge, a dark spot, top of a cupboard). Fill the flasks with warm water. ⚠ SAFETY The water should be no more than hand hot. Label and cover the outside of the plastic beakers, each with a different material.

What to do
Demonstrate how to read a thermometer. Ask pairs of children to read the thermometers placed around the classroom. Experiment by holding the thermometer under a cold running tap and then find the reading. List noon temperatures for last week. (Ensure the figures differ.) Show how to record this changing information in a line graph, so the children become familiar with this form of recording data.

Then explain your problem: your warm drink, once out of your thermos flask, goes cold quickly at playtime in your beaker. Your beaker needs the best insulating material to keep your drink warm for as long as possible. Organise small groups (pairs or threes, depending on your resources), giving each group a thermometer and beaker. Encourage groups to talk about their material and predict its performance as an insulator. Check and record on the board the temperature of the water while in the flask; then pour it into the beakers. Keep the test fair by putting the same amount of liquid into each beaker.

At two-minute intervals, ask the groups to check and record their water temperature. Do this for 14 minutes. How do the final readings compare with the predictions? Now the groups should convert their information to a line graph (they could use a computer data-handling package). What deductions can they make from the graph?

Special support
You may need to *engage attention* carefully for a child with cognition and learning needs so that they begin to focus on tiny detail. *Keep it concrete* by setting up a personally meaningful situation in which the child can safely feel or experience the temperature as well as record it.

Extension
Consider how to keep ice cream from melting for as long as possible.

AGE RANGE
Nine to eleven.

GROUP SIZE
Whole group, in pairs.

LEARNING OBJECTIVE FOR ALL THE CHILDREN
● To learn how to measure their pulse rate and relate it to heartbeat.

INDIVIDUAL LEARNING TARGET
● To work with a partner to log simple data using ICT.

Finger on the pulse

Using ICT to log data can make a scientific investigation motivating and productive.

What you need
One-minute timers or watches with a second hand (one per two children); computers (preferably one per pair).

Preparation
Practise locating your pulse, by placing two fingers on the inside of your wrist or the side of your neck, and using a computer data-handling program or spreadsheet for constructing bar charts.

What to do
Talk about the relationship between heartbeat and pulse: pulse rate tells you how many times the heart beats per minute. Let the children watch as you sit down and relax. Then, with a watch or timer clearly visible, take your resting pulse rate. Count the beats of your heart for one minute and then record your result on the board.

Practise locating pulses with the class. Give each pair of children a timer for them to measure and record their resting pulse rates. Let the class watch as you remeasure and record your pulse rate again. Has it changed? (Hopefully!) Discuss likely reasons. (You may have been more active.) Explain that our pulses vary even with little or no change of activity. Ask the children to make and record their own second measurements.

Now work through a number of one-minute activities that vary in pace. For example: chatting to a friend; helping to tidy-up the classroom; copying a display heading in perfect writing; testing strength and grip against a partner; sitting completely still. Between activities, wait one minute and then ask for measurements to be taken and recorded. Periodically, retake and record your own.

Discuss your set of results. Explain that variation in a person's resting pulse rate is always likely. Decide on the most accurate measurement for you, perhaps you had the same recording twice, or choose a number in the middle of your results. Write this on the board. Ask partners to help each other decide on a single result. Write these (one measurement per child) on the board, or type and photocopy a list. Let the children enter this data on a computer program and produce bar charts. Can the children answer your questions? For example, 'What was the highest pulse rate?'

Special support
Use *adult support* to take the pulse of any children who have difficulties.

Extension
Find out about hearts and circulation – why does a healthy heart help us to stay fit?

AGE RANGE
Nine to eleven.

GROUP SIZE
Whole group, small groups.

LEARNING OBJECTIVE FOR ALL THE CHILDREN
● To make and record comparisons of how different surfaces reflect light and to draw conclusions from their comparisons.

INDIVIDUAL LEARNING TARGET
● To observe and talk about a simple effect.

What can you see?

This activity helps children draw conclusions from their findings and begin to make predictions about what might happen next.

What you need
A collection of shiny and dull surfaces (for example: mirrors, cutlery, paper, plastic, glass, foil, matt and gloss painted areas, polished wood); torches (one per three or four children); pens and paper.

Preparation
Identify examples of shiny or dull surfaces in the school.

What to do
Let the children work in small groups. Explain that they are going to investigate dull and shiny surfaces. Identify some examples – perhaps a wall, a door or a specific pane of glass in the school. Give each group a selection of objects or materials, some with dull surfaces, some with shiny surfaces; or have display areas for the groups to visit in turn. Ask the children to first predict and then test which of the surfaces reflect a torch beam and which surfaces they can see themselves in. Suggest that the children present their work in the form of a table with these headings: *surface, material, prediction, test result, comment.*

Afterwards, ask the children, individually, to make a study of their results table, and identify conclusions that can be made. Then, re-forming in their small groups, they should pose questions for one another. For example: 'Which type of surface reflects light best?'; 'Which type of surface can be used as a mirror?' The group must then agree on a piece of information about one of the materials that they will present to the class.

Come together as a class to share these conclusions. What conclusions are most important? Agree on a list. In particular, make sure that the children have recognised that the shiny materials meet both demands: they reflect a torch beam and reflections can be seen in them. Take the activity further by asking each group to compile a list of the everyday uses of mirrors. Share ideas and create a class display featuring the varied uses of mirrors in everyday life.

Special support
Make sure that the child with cognition and learning needs is fully included and has a definite job to do. *Keep it concrete* by involving them in the practical side of the activity and *alter the pace* if necessary so that they have time to respond and draw simple conclusions.

Extension
Investigate which materials reflect or absorb heat and record the findings.

HISTORY

The strand of history has been chosen to serve as an example of how to plan and adapt activities to support children with cognition and learning needs. Though they may well experience learning difficulties across all of the humanities, it is hoped that examples in this section will provide you with the starting points and ideas necessary for helping you deliver the humanities curriculum in a supportive and inclusive way. Use your creativity to design activities that appeal to all learning styles, *keeping it concrete* with plenty to look at, listen to and interact with. If your topic can be introduced in the first person, then this will encourage involvement and understanding from children who are still at an early stage of their learning. Dress up, use role play, try small-world play, enjoy pictures, explore artefacts and imagine yourselves in the 'there and then'. All this helps you to *extend imagination*, make use of *play power* and ensure *appropriate content* for children with cognition and learning needs.

At KS1, all children can be helped to make comparisons and see differences between then and now, especially if you make use of real artefacts. Some children with cognition and learning needs might find the vocabulary involved in describing the past tense hard, but you might find you can *teach reading to improve language*. History provides opportunities for teaching *sequence* and you will probably find that giving a child picture sequences to arrange in order will help them sequence their history ideas or talking and writing. Use *mind mapping* and *mnemonics* to *improve memory skills* and try to include activities that involve personal memories within the children's or their parents' lifetimes.

By KS2, most children will be beginning to place events, people and changes into correct periods of time. This becomes easier for the child with cognition and learning needs if you can *keep it concrete* by using visual time lines on the wall. Making sense of

historical data involves abstract and complex thinking, yet children can help each other at many levels of ability to gather information, explore data and present or describe what they have found out. Small-group work, the strategic use of a *key worker* or support assistant and the use of *peer support* all make this kind of activity more inclusive. Above all, history can be an intrinsic motivator – use your imagination, enthusiasm and flexibility to make it fun for everyone, whatever their level of ability.

AGE RANGE
Five to seven.

GROUP SIZE
Whole group, in pairs.

LEARNING OBJECTIVE FOR ALL THE CHILDREN
● To learn about some of the improvements made by Florence Nightingale, and to identify some reasons for her actions.

INDIVIDUAL LEARNING TARGET
● To take part in a themed activity linked to Florence Nightingale.

A lady with a lamp

This activity uses role play to encourage the children to experience history first-hand.

What you need
Enlarged copy of photocopiable page 93.

Preparation
Find out about Florence Nightingale: a 19th century British nurse who cared deeply about poverty and healthcare. She nursed the sick and needy, particularly during the Crimean War. She was sent in 1854 by the British Government to take charge of the army hospital for wounded soldiers in Scutari, Turkey, which had terrible conditions.

What to do
Tell the children the story of Florence Nightingale. Point out that she was used to clean, tidy hospitals in London with good patient care. Highlight some of the problems in Scutari: chaotic, filthy conditions; rubbish; rats; dirty bedding; no pillows; poor hygiene; shortages of medicine, dressings, bandages; and dark, gloomy wards.

As you focus on details, involve the children by allocating talk partners. Give them short situations to role play. For example: *Become Florence Nightingale and one of her nurses. You have just arrived in Scutari hospital. What do you say to each other?*

Having highlighted the problems that were in the hospital, ask the children to suggest improvements. Display the picture of the hospital at Scutari using photocopiable page 93 and agree on a list of changes that Florence Nightingale made:
● cleaning and scrubbing wards
● improving hygiene
● reducing germs
● washing bedlinen
● sending for extra supplies of medicine and food
● dressing wounds, bandaging patients
● organising the large kitchen
● making wards lighter, by carrying a lamp at night.
Ask partners to role play important characters (Florence Nightingale, a doctor, patient or nurse) and to talk about some of these changes (Florence asking an army official for more supplies; Florence talking to a patient). Move among the class, prompting conversations. Let some children share their role play with the whole class.

Special support
Keep role-play activities short, simple and concrete so that children build-up confidence and do not run out of things to say.

Extension
Write a letter home from a wounded soldier in the hospital in Scutari. What did it feel like to be there?

AGE RANGE
Five to seven.

GROUP SIZE
Whole group.

LEARNING OBJECTIVE FOR ALL THE CHILDREN
● To find out about seaside holidays in the past by asking questions of an adult visitor.

INDIVIDUAL LEARNING TARGET
● To use or respond to language in the past tense.

Seaside memories

This activity helps children use their own memories to think about the past.

What you need
A small suitcase with modern items or pictures from your summer holiday last year (for example: sunglasses, sunhat, sun cream, flip-flops, swimsuit, goggles, flippers).

Preparation
Prepare appropriate seaside information for your answers when you act as a visitor later in the lesson. Display key question words: *Where? What? Why? When? Who?*

What to do
Display the contents of your suitcase. Encourage the children to question you about the sort of place you went to. Prompt the use of past-tense verbs. Reveal that you went on a seaside holiday.

Give further practice in using the past tense, by asking the children, in pairs, to spend a few minutes in imaginative discussion about a seaside holiday they took together last year. Then snowball into fours, as one pair takes turns to question the other pair about last year's holiday. Move among groups, checking that everyone contributes and uses the past tense. Let the whole class hear some of the questions and answers.

Suggest travelling further back in time. What would they ask one of your grandparents about seaside holidays in their childhood? Divide the seaside subject into areas: *Places* (near and far away); *Travel* (cars, planes and trains); *Amusements* (shows, funfairs, rides, slot machines, piers); *Clothes* (swimsuits, size, material, comfort); *Adults* (enjoyment, clothes); *Sun* (sunglasses, tan, sun cream, protection); *Sea* (flippers, snorkel, goggles).

Assign partners a subject area. Ask them to help each other to make up a question to ask the future visitor. Remind them that that they must use the past tense.

Now your visitor (you in disguise!) arrives. Even a small addition to your clothes – a wig or different jacket – will remind the children of your new identity. Introduce yourself and answer the children's questions, adding information not revealed by the questions. Were seaside holidays better then or now?

Special support
Speaking in the past tense is hard for many children with learning needs. If a phrase is incorrect, simply repeat it back correctly to the child and move on. You can then use *adult support* to work on this individually or in a small group, using prompting.

Extension
Make and write postcards from travellers in days gone by.

AGE RANGE
Seven to nine.

GROUP SIZE
Whole group.

LEARNING OBJECTIVE FOR ALL THE CHILDREN
● To learn how many times Henry VIII married.

INDIVIDUAL LEARNING TARGET
● To use a simple time line to sequence events.

Time lines

In this activity children make a simple time line.

What you need
Dates of the marriages of Henry VIII; paper for individual time lines; pencils and pens.

Preparation
Decide on the size and time extent of the children's time lines.

What to do
Talk to the children about a time line. Stress that this is a clear way to display and sequence events. Collaborate on a class model, using shared experiences, perhaps focusing on a relatively short period of time, such as the previous term. Which month should start the time line? Which month goes at the end? Agree on important class or school events that occurred during that time period (for example, sports day). Are there other events important to individual children?

Demonstrate how you decide where to place the event. Precise dates are not essential – knowing even the approximate date allows you to place the event sensibly on the time line. (For example, the carol service is positioned near the end of the line because it was near the end of term.) Explain that a time line needs to be clear, so arrows could indicate points on the line and the writing could be kept well away. Symbols and keys could be useful.

Ask the children to use this format to show the chronology of the marriages of Henry VIII. Revise the facts, listing names and marriage dates, but in random order. For example:
● marriage dates: Anne of Cleves – 1540, Jane Seymour – 1536, Catherine Parr – 1543, Catherine Howard – 1540, Anne Boleyn – 1533, Catherine of Aragon – 1509
● death of Henry VIII: 1547.
Agree with the children on the period that the time line should cover, perhaps from the date of Henry's first marriage up to his death. Decide on the size of the time line, and help the children to relate the size to the period of time covered. Suggest working lightly in pencil before producing a final version, with all the dates in chronological order. Remind them to avoid overcrowding on the time line by using arrows, small pictures, coloured symbols, numbers or letters. A key can be provided underneath. Display the results.

Special support
Sequencing can be difficult for children with cognition and learning needs. *Keep it concrete* and provide an *alternative means of recording* by giving the child pictures to stick along the time line, numbered in order from one to six for the six wives.

Extension
Children could make time lines of the key events in their own lives.

AGE RANGE
Seven to nine.

GROUP SIZE
Whole group, small groups.

LEARNING OBJECTIVE FOR ALL THE CHILDREN
● To conduct a Viking case study.

INDIVIDUAL LEARNING TARGET
● To work with a partner in collecting data via a website.

The Vikings are here!

The *use of ICT* assists historical enquiry in this activity.

What you need
Computers (one per small group or pair); materials for a class display; paper and pens.

Preparation
Choose suitable websites about the Vikings, such as: www.bbc.co.uk/ schools/vikings and www.bbc.co.uk/history/ancient/vikings/.

What to do
Explain that you want the children to do a class study of the Vikings: people who invaded and settled in Britain in the past. Suggest the use of internet websites for research. Investigate the layout of a website used on a previous occasion. Demonstrate important ICT skills: locating and opening a site, using hyperlinks, scrolling and moving between windows.

Explain that you want the children to work on different areas of the Viking case study. Agree on a list of questions or areas, for example: *Who were the Vikings?; When and why did they invade Britain?; Means of travel; Where they settled; How they lived; Clothes; Beliefs; Trade; Exploration; What happened to the Vikings?*

Suggest websites that will be useful. (Limiting the choice to sites that you know are manageable will help children with difficulties.) Allocate subject areas and divide the children into small groups. Explain that you want each group to contribute to a class display on this case study. Talk about how information is presented in museums and emphasise audience appeal. Explain that research results can be presented in a variety of ways: written text; maps; diagrams; pictures; short audiotapes. Provide working tips such as:
● deciding what needs to be found out
● taking turns using the computer mouse or keyboard
● making brief notes
● making rough sketches and diagrams
● reading parts of the screen aloud to one another (a help to children with reading problems).
Encourage the children to make notes that they will write up later in their own words. The group will need one or more sessions to complete their research and collaborate on the presentation. Give every group an opportunity to present their findings to the class.

Special support
Look for an *alternative means of recording*, perhaps with the child dictating rough notes to a *learning mentor* or partner.

Extension
Write and publish the 'Viking News' as a way of bringing together all your findings.

AGE RANGE
Nine to eleven.

GROUP SIZE
Whole group.

LEARNING OBJECTIVE FOR ALL THE CHILDREN
● To find out about important figures in Victorian times and to present their findings in different ways.

INDIVIDUAL LEARNING TARGET
● To work with an adult to produce a mind map about the Victorians.

Memory mind maps

This activity uses *mind mapping* to help the children to recall, select and organise historical information.

What you need
Individual copies of photocopiable page 94; one copy for OHP of photocopiable page 69; written history texts; rough paper; large paper for the children's mind maps; pencils and coloured pens.

Preparation
Make a mind map of the information in a written history text.

What to do
Remind the children of the format of a mind map. A mind map can be a useful way not just to plan a piece of writing but also to remind you of what you know. On an OHP, view photocopiable page 69, reminding the children that short branches are subsidiary to long branches, and writing size indicates relative word importance.

Show the children some history texts, pointing out that many of them require a lot of reading. Ask if they could produce a summary of a text in the form of a mind map. It would use key words and would remind them quickly of important facts. Model an example, reading the children a short history text and then condensing the main points into a mind map.

Now give the children copies of photocopiable page 94, suggesting that they read it with a partner. Allow five to ten minutes for them to absorb the information. List and display the names, key words or difficult spellings on the board. The children, working with partners or individually, must produce a mind map of the information. If remembering the content is too difficult, let the children use the text for reference. Suggest that they plan the mind map in rough first. Emphasise the importance of deciding on a central word and working outwards, always thinking about where a branch should lead.

For final versions, encourage the children to use large sheets of paper. Suggest using different colours to distinguish one set of branches from another. Point out the benefit of adding some pictures and the need to use different writing sizes. Let the children act as testers for one another. How good are the maps at jogging their memories about the text?

Special support
Use *appropriate content* and *check level* for a child with difficulties. For example, you could simplify the text on the photocopiable sheet covering just the paragraph on Victoria's family life.

Extension
Try drawing a mind map using information sourced from a simple illustrated reference book.

AGE RANGE
Nine to eleven.

GROUP SIZE
Whole group, small groups.

LEARNING OBJECTIVE FOR ALL THE CHILDREN
● To learn in what ways the modern Olympic games are like the ancient ones.

INDIVIDUAL LEARNING TARGET
● To collect information about an event that happened in the past.

Time travellers

Looking at a popular topic such as sports, both in the past and the present, will be personally meaningful for most children and can be used to focus and motivate them.

What you need
Resource material (books or websites); computers (one per pair or small group).

Preparation
Familiarise yourself with the internet websites you plan to use: www.bbc.co.uk/schools/ancientgreece/olympia is excellent. Decide on a list of topic areas linked to the ancient Olympic games.

What to do
Present the scenario: the children have used a time machine to travel back to the city of Olympia in ancient Greece. They want to find out how the ancient Olympic games compares with their modern one.

Set up small discussion groups, asking them to list three or four topics that they want to ask the ancient Greeks about. Encourage the children to list subject areas, not questions (for example, *Sportswomen*). Share the results, letting each group offer its list. Write the ideas on the board and consider the complete results. Is there repetition? Have important areas been left out?

Work together condensing ideas into a manageable list, including perhaps: the place; the sporting events; the competitors; the spectators; and similar festivals. Make sure that your list matches information available in your resource material. Leave only the agreed headings on the board.

Meeting a person from ancient Greece, each time traveller must have a question (about one of these things) ready. What will they ask? Suggest that pairs or small groups of children work together to decide on the best wording for a question each. Encourage trial and error, as the children draft and make final written questions.

Make your resources available. Invite the children to discuss and make notes as they gather information from pictures as well as texts. Afterwards they can work on the wording of the answers that the ancient Greeks would give, perhaps using role play to answer one another's questions. What did the time travellers find out? Were the games of ancient Greece very different from today's Olympic games?

Special support
Partner or group support will help children with difficulties. Focus on helping the child to gather information. Keep comparisons *concrete*, perhaps using real artefacts and pictures to make differences stand out.

Extension
Explore different ways of presenting your comparative information, for example, visual charts that show 'now' and 'then'.

Florence Nightingale

Queen Victoria

Victoria was Queen of the United Kingdom for over 60 years. She was known for her strong sense of duty and her determination to live her life according to a strong moral code. She had a strong influence on 19th century British attitudes and behaviour.

Victoria was born in 1819. At that time, the British Empire extended to countries all over the world: at 18, Victoria became Queen of Britain and this vast empire.

Victoria enjoyed great popularity as queen. In 1840 she married her cousin, Prince Albert. Victoria and Albert shared a strong sense of responsibility to their subjects and they were both respected for their high standards of behaviour.

Large families were usual in the 19th century, and Victoria and Albert had nine children. It was a very happy marriage and, when Albert died in 1861, Victoria became depressed. For many years she withdrew from public life. The public grew restless and the Queen's popularity decreased. Fortunately, in later years, Victoria's energy and enthusiasm for public duty returned. As her people saw more of her, so her popularity returned.

In 1901, after the longest reign of any British monarch, Victoria died. She was succeeded by her son, Edward VII.

RECOMMENDED RESOURCES

GOVERNMENT GUIDANCE
● DfEE: Supporting the Target Setting Process (ref DfEE 0065/2001) – all about P scales.
● DfES: Special Educational Needs Code of Practice (ref DfES 581/2001).
● DfES: SEN Toolkit (ref 0558/2001).
● DfES: Inclusive Schooling: Children with Special Educational Needs (ref 0774/2001).
● DfES: The National Literacy and Numeracy Strategies: Including All Children in the Literacy Hour and Daily Mathematics Lesson (ref 0465/2002).
● QCA: Planning, Teaching and Assessing the Curriculum for Pupils with Learning Difficulties (2001).
● The Government initiative 'Removing Barriers to Achievement' can be obtained from www.standards.dfes.gov.uk.

NATIONAL ORGANISATIONS
● Alliance for Inclusive Education: Unit 2, 70 South Lambeth Road, London SW8 1RL. Tel: 020 77355277. (Campaigns to end compulsory segregation of children with special education needs within the education system.)
● Barnardo's: Tanners Lane, Barkingside, Ilford, Essex IG6 1QG.
Tel: 020 85508822. Fax: 020 85516870. Website: www.barnardos.org.uk.
(Provides care and support for children in need and their families, with projects throughout the UK.) Send for their publication list: Barnado's Child Care Publications (address as above).
● Children in Scotland (training and information on services): Princes House, 5 Shandwick Place, Edinburgh EH2 4RG. Website: www.childreninscotland.org.uk.

● Contact a Family: 209–211 City Road, London EC1V 1JN. Website: www.cafamily.org.uk. (Produces on subscription the 'CaF Directory: Specific Conditions, Rare Disorders and UK Family Support Groups'.)
● The Department for Education and Skills (DfES) (for parent information and for Government circulars and advice including the SEN Code of Practice). Website: www.dfes.gov.uk.
● The Down's Syndrome Association: website: www.dsa-uk.com.
● Makaton Vocabulary Development Project: 31 Firwood Drive, Camberley, Surrey GU15 3QD. (Information about Makaton sign vocabulary and training.) Website: www.makaton.org.
● MENCAP: www.mencap.org.uk. (Support organisation for children with severe learning difficulties and their families.)
● National Association for Special Educational Needs: NASEN House, 4/5 Amber Business Village, Amber Close, Amington, Tamworth, Staffordshire B77 4RP. Tel: 01827 311500. Fax: 01827 313005. Email: welcome@nasen.org.uk. Website: www.nasen.org.uk. (Professional association with a database of relevant courses for those wishing to train in SEN; also runs training courses itself.)
● National Children's Bureau: 8 Wakley Street, London EC1V 7QE. Tel: 020 78436000, 020 78436008 (library enquiry line: 10am–12 noon, and 2–4pm). Email: library@ncb.org.uk. Website: www.ncb.org.uk. (A multidisciplinary organisation concerned with the promotion and identification of the interests of all children and young people. Involved in

research, policy and practice development, and consultancy.)

USEFUL RESOURCES

● Acorn Educational Ltd: 32 Queen Eleanor Road, Geddington, Kettering, Northants NN14 1AY. Tel: 01536 400212. Website: www.acorneducational.co.uk. (Equipment and resources including special needs.)

● Anything Left-handed Ltd: 57 Brewer Street, London W1F 9UL. Tel: 020 74373910. Website: www.anything left-handed.co.uk.

● 'Effective Teaching and Learning in the Primary Classroom – a Practical Guide to Brain Compatible Learning' by Sara Shaw and Trevor Hawes, Optimal Learning series. Available from Optimal Learning: 8 Dover Street, Kibworth Beauchamp, Leicester LE8 0HD. Tel: 0116 279111. Website: www.optimal-learning.net.

● Fisher-Marriott Software: 58 Victoria Road, Woodbridge IP12 1EL. Tel: 01394 387050. Website: www.fishermarriott.com. (For literacy ICT resources such as 'Starspell'.)

● The 'Index for Inclusion: Developing Learning and Participation in Schools' by T. Booth and M. Ainscow can be obtained from CSIE (Centre for Studies on Inclusive Education): New Redland, Frenchay Campus, Coldharbour Lane, Bristol BS16 1QU. Website: www.csie.org.uk

● Don Johnston Special Needs: 18/19 Clarendon Court, Calver Road, Winwick Quay, Warrington WA2 8QP. Website: www.donjohnston.co.uk. (Specialist in intervention resources.)

● KCS: FREEPOST, Southampton SO17 1YA. (Specialist tools for making computer equipment accessible to all children.)

● LDA Primary and Special Needs catalogue: Abbeygate House, East Road, Cambridge CB1 1DB. Tel: 0845 1204776. Website: www.ldalearning.com. (For example, the Jenny Mosley 'Circle Time Kit' with puppets, rainstick, magician's cloak and many props for making circle time motivating.)

● 'The Learning Gym – Fun-to-Do Activities for Success at School' by Erich Ballinger (Brain Gym), also available from Optimal Learning (see above).

● nfer Nelson produces a 'Specialist

Assessments for Learning Support' catalogue. Tel: 0845 6021937. Website: www.nfer-nelson.co.uk.

● PIVATS: www.lancashire.gov.uk/ education/advisory/index.shtml.

● The Psychological Corporation produces a catalogue of 'Educational Assessment & Intervention' resources. Tel: 01865 888188. Website: www.harcourt-uk.com.

● SBS (Step by Step): customer careline 0845 1252550. (Toys and equipment for all special needs.)

● White Space Ltd: 41 Mall Road, London W6 9DG. Tel 020 87485927. Website: www.wordshark.co.uk. (For literacy ICT resources such as the 'Wordshark' software.)

● Winslow produces an 'Education & Special Needs' catalogue. Tel: 0845 2302777. Website: www.winslow-cat.com.